The Bride

Arising

A Vision of a Bridal

Journey

**By: Carolyn "Charismata"
Weaver**

The Bride Arising

Cover Design by Paul Weaver
Cover Artwork and Chapter Illustrations by Judith Kayadoe with
Royalty Fine Art
Vision Artwork by Carolyn Weaver
Copyright © 2022 Carolyn "Charismata" Weaver -BH Publishing
Printed in the United States of America
All rights reserved.
ISBN: 978-1-7349297-3-7 (Paperback)

DEDICATION

*This book is dedicated to my mother who is now
in the arms of her Bridegroom, Jesus Christ.*

ACKNOWLEDGEMENTS

One of my goals in the process of this book has been to include other voices for it to be a fuller picture of what it means to be in this place of preparation as the Bride. I'm so grateful for those who have been willing to come along side of me on this project offering support, words, and insight.

To my husband, who became my graphic designer for the cover, thank you for all the times you have said yes to me offering your trust in me. I love you!

To my three girls, my highest hope for you is to say a resounding "Yes" to your Bridegroom, King Jesus.

To my mom who went home to meet her Bridegroom before the completion of this book. I love you. I know you are singing a new song with Jesus in heaven now.

To my family and friends, who patient allow me to process things out as I'm finishing yet another project, your support means so much.

To all those voices who have offered me suggestions, editorial help, context, and your support, you know who you are, and I am forever grateful.

To my best friend, my Bridegroom, Jesus Christ, you are everything to me. May my answer always be "Yes".

FOREWORD

Each person's life journey, as they go from darkness to light, from encumberment to freedom, requires profound transformation. This is true for every single human being. Entering the presence, the holiness, of the living God, all that is not of the Lord surfaces to be burned away. Some life journeys appear more challenging than others, even appearing daunting from the outside. But each of us has been designed for Christ's victory over the challenges that come our way. As we reach deeper and higher into God's glory, His sweet victorious presence becomes ours.

Carolyn's journey may seem daunting to some. Although she does not give any details of her life, she gives enough impression, throughout her healing journey, that we can imagine where she began. But because of her joy in the Lord and His manifest glory in the pages of this book, The Bride Arising is highly inspirational. It will encourage you and challenge you towards greater intimacy with God.

Each and every one of us can take our own GOD-crafted Bridal journey with Jesus, coming into the purity of His embrace and the holiness of His marriage covenant with His church and its members. No one is excluded for any reason whatsoever except for their own choice. Thus, The Bride Arising is a book to cherish, to read repeatedly, to ponder, and to take seriously. Carolyn's journey can become a launching pad for you to discover more about your own. Be blessed!

Wendy Cohen, Author of
"FREEDOM: True Freedom Lasts Forever",
"The Waters of Life", and "Adonai Keeps His Promise"
https://houseofbeauty.org

TABLE OF CONTENTS

INTRODUCTION

"Arise, my dearest. Hurry, my darling. Come away with me! I have come as you have asked to draw you to my heart and lead you out. For now is the time, my beautiful one. The season has changed, the bondage of your barren winter has ended, and the season of hiding is over and gone." Song of Songs 2:10-11 TPT

Can you feel it? Do you sense something shaking, awakening, like a giant from its slumber? As the Bride awakes and shakes herself from her slumbered state, the ground quakes in anticipation of a resurrection. She wipes the sleep from her eyes and arises to meet her beloved Bridegroom.

For several years, the Holy Spirit has prodded me about the season of preparation we are currently in as the Bride of Christ. Relentlessly, God is focused on preparing the Bride for the coming of the Bridegroom.

As a whole, the Bride has seemingly been unaware of her slumbered state - asleep in the light. The Bridegroom knocks on the door of her heart, yearning for her to wake up and to let Him in, so that He can prepare her for Him only - for her wedding day.

The clarion call is for the Bride to Arise.

This book unfolds a prophetic vision that the Lord Jesus Christ revealed to me several years ago regarding this preparation. To this day, this experience of encountering Jesus as my Bridegroom has been one of the most intense, intimate, and revelatory visions I've ever had.

The vision you are about to read unexpectedly occurred at a women's conference some years ago in a prayer room that had been set up for participants to engage in reflective prayer with the Lord. The intercessory team borrowed a huge cloth from another prayer ministry that had a labyrinth drawn on it and placed the cloth in the middle of floor of the prayer room.

A labyrinth is simply a tool that has been used throughout history for different purposes. In church history, it primarily functioned as a mediative prayer

2

journey or walk. In this case, the prayer team's goal was for women to prayerfully walk the circular pathway to the center of the labyrinth for the purpose of experiencing a deeper connection with God. (Further history of the labyrinth is included in "The Bridal Backstory".)

In sharing this vision with you, my uttermost desire is for you to experience Jesus as your Bridegroom. This is both an individual experience and a corporate experience, which I explain more about in the Bridal Backstory – Who is the Bride.

Everyone has different strengths in perceiving God, but as it says in John 10:27, the sheep know the Shepherd's voice; therefore, I firmly believe that if you have a relationship with God through Jesus, His Son, then you are able to hear from Him. That may come through visions, dreams, reading His Word, hearing His voice within you, artistic expression, music, etc. I will explain this more in the second section of this book, where I will share some exercises to help you to engage with the Trinity for yourself.

This is not meant to be a how to book – a check off list of things to do to prepare yourself as the Bride.

3

Though there can be steps to help a relationship to be healthy, this book is meant to show relationship as fluid, living, intimate, and growing. Healthy relationship must begin with a foundation of trust. I hope as you read through the vision, you will be able to see yourself on the bridal journey, both individually and corporately (as being a part of the Body of Christ) as He makes us ready for the wedding day.

Relax and take Jesus by the hand, as you walk side by side with your Bridegroom on a bridal journey - a vision of the Bride Arising.

THE BRIDAL VISION - SPRING 2016

"Come Meet with Me"

"If I go to the prayer room now, it will be filled with people," I twisted the napkin in my hand while eating lunch with my friend. "Maybe I just won't go," I sighed. My friend's eyebrows rose.

"Come on. You know you want to go," she continued. "There have been some amazing encounters with the Lord already." We continued to debate back and forth, until I finally concluded in my mind that I would get up extra early the last morning and sneak in before anyone else would be awake.

Just as if an alarm clock had rung in my ears, my eyes popped open well before the sun rose. I rolled over to pick up my phone. At first my eyesight blurred, as I rubbed the sleep from them. 5:55 am. Wide-awake, I lumbered to a sitting position. "Well, I guess, Lord, we are going to the prayer room."

Silently, I rolled out of bed, tiptoed across the room, and slipped out the door so as not to awaken my roommate. I continued down the hall to the prayer room like a mouse making a midnight patrol.

Soft music greeted me as the door creaked lightly when I peeked in. "Oh good, no one is here yet," I whispered to myself.

Inwardly, my thoughts tumbled. "Why do I feel so vulnerable?" "Should I text my friend, so she can come pray with me as I walk the labyrinth?" "No. No. It's too early." I battled with myself, as I approached the great maze on the floor.

"This is silly," my heart raced with anticipation, yet I wasn't sure why.

I heard a whisper in my heart, "Come meet with me."

My legs shook, as I lifted my leaded foot to the starting point of the labyrinth.

Immediately, I went into the clearest, open vision I've ever seen to this point in my life.

The Exchange

The Bridegroom, Jesus Christ, met me, gently taking me by the arm, guiding me forward. His kind eyes overwhelmed me as He said, "My Beloved. I'm so glad you came. We are going on a bridal journey."

The first thing I noticed was how handsome, gentle, and kind He is. His immense beauty - the crystal, endless tenderness in His eyes - like an ocean of love I could drown in - overwhelmed me.

As He turned to face me, He said, "My Love, I believe it's time to get dressed."

A wave of horror overtook me as I looked down at my attire. I desperately attempted to smooth out my muddied and torn clothes that I was wearing. With a cloak of fear clutched around my neck, I wanted to hide my dress of shame, but there was nowhere to run. When you are used to wearing such things, you hardly notice, until the light shines on it.

Seeming to perceive my discomfort, compassion filled Jesus's face.

"It's OK, Dear One. I already brought your new dress for you, and it's fitted perfectly to you," He paused. "You'll love it." His eyes glistened with the element of surprise and anticipation.

An angel appeared behind Him, holding up the most gorgeous dress I've ever seen.

My mind flashed back to the day when I had found my wedding dress that I wore on the day I married my husband. I had been a Christian schoolteacher at the time and had a small savings to work with for our wedding day. I walked into a thrift store with my mom just to see if they might have something, and on the rack was the most beautiful dress – perfect for me. It didn't even need one alteration. I knew that dress was a kiss from God.

Yet, this dress that Jesus presented me was way beyond anything I could have ever imagined. It emanated a glowing, warm light, and was interlaced with diamonds and embroidered with patterns of roses.

"Daughter, it's time to get dressed. May I take your old garments now?"

My mind reeled. "I can't let Him see my nakedness." A prickly feeling began to crawl up my legs, then numbness until it reached my tightening chest. "Breathe. Just breathe."

Opening my eyes, I quickly looked around the prayer room. Everything was still there. The table sat with communion elements across the room, a book lay open of prayers from St. Patrick, and the cloth with the labyrinth drawn on it was still under my feet.

I sighed deeply. "This all seems so real, Lord." I stared up into the artificial light in the prayer room, as my heart beat slowed to the calm rhythm of the music.

"Daughter, I must remove the old before you take on the new. I promise not to expose you. I will not expose my Bride. I cover you with my robe of righteousness," He said. His words were so gentle, "Yet, you will have to trust me, and let me take the old garment for you to go forward."

I still hesitated, but it's like He knew my fears, and yet was unmoved by them. His love is relentless in pursuing our hearts.

"Beloved, I want to exchange wedding gifts with you," Jesus said.

My eyes widened, "With me, Lord?"

"Isn't it customary?" He winked at me; besides I have some very special gifts for you, but first, your garments."

"But I don't have anything to give to you."

"Oh, yes you do," His eyes fell on the wad of dirty clothes that now filled my arms. "Will you allow me to take that now and show you the gifts?"

"It's not that I don't want the gifts, Lord," I bowed my head staring at my feet. I realized for the first time I was wrapped in a robe that felt warm and cozy, like a holy hug.

"I know you don't feel you deserve them, child. But sweetheart, do any of my children deserve anything? My love is a gift freely given with no strings attached. It is not deserved or earned. It is simply given to anyone who will receive it."

"The garments, please?"

Reluctantly, I placed them into a box that an angel was holding in front of me. The Lord closed the lid down tight on the box, locking it. Swiftly, the angel removed it.

The First Gift

"Now, my Lovely One, may I present your wedding gifts?"

I nodded my head up and down.

"Good," He said as He clapped His hands.

Another angel appeared with a small, silver box. With a bow, he presented it to the Bridegroom.

"For you," He said as He gingerly placed the gift in my hands.

My hands trembled as I held it, fumbled as I lifted the lid. Dazzled, my eyes blinked in amazement at an engagement ring. Light shot out of it like a radiant rainbow, sending beams of color reflecting off of the many facets of the intricately cut diamond, set in stunning gold. Around the gem in the middle, was laid a rainbow of twelve stones set in a circle - the stones of the priest.

I gasped, "This is too much." I stumbled over my words, "Too much." I turned my eyes away from the ring. "I just can't accept this."

Immediately, I could tell I had wounded the Lord's feelings. His tone was filled with hurt. "You don't like it? You don't accept it? You don't accept me?"

My heart welled with conflicting emotions. "Oh, I don't know what to do?" I shuffled my feet. "This gift is just too good for me." His words about not deserving anything shot across my mind.

"My Love, look at me. Just look into my eyes, My Bride." He gently tipped my chin up, so my eyes met His. It wasn't rejection, like I expected, but pure love. "Listen to my words. Let them go deep. There is nothing, nothing in heaven or earth I would not give to you. I have already given you my very life. This is the engagement ring I designed perfectly for you. Will you accept it from me?"

"Oh, Jesus! Yes, I accept."

He gently slipped it on my trembling finger, and then kissed my cheek.

Tears streamed down my face, as He handed me a handkerchief embroidered on the edges with gold to wipe them away.

The Bath

"Sweetheart, before you put the dress on, I must wash you," He said. "I know this feels uncomfortable, but remember when I said I would not expose you. My love protects you. It covers you." The intensity of His eyes made me wince. "Beloved, my love will not rape you."

My cheeks flushed red with heat. My heart beat wildly pulsing in my neck.

"I have no desire to take from you. My love doesn't take, doesn't steal, and doesn't violate your free will. I will not rape My Bride," His voice broke with pain. "I will never treat you as others have." He gently took my hands in His.

"Please, My Love, let me wash you. I will ask your permission again as we need to wash each part of you. And I promise, I will cover your vulnerability. Will you trust me?"

As I consented, an angel appeared with a bronze bowl of water and a towel draped over one arm. Respectfully, Jesus washed each part of me. As He did, I could feel the pain, the shame, the fears, the lies, and the anger lifting. Meticulously, He dabbed at deep, oozing gashes. As He did, He applied a soothing healing ointment.

"From the trees by the river of life," He said as He smiled. He didn't seem to tire from His work, but began to whistle as He wrapped gauze around each wound. "There. That's better." He grinned as He winked at me.

"One last place to go," He got down on His hands and knees with the wash pan in front of Him. "Please sit here," He pointed behind to where a chair had been placed.

"My feet, Lord, oh, not my feet," I protested. "That's just too much. They stink." The heat raced to my face again, and it felt like my head would pop like a can of Coke shaken.

"Yes, dear, I must wash your feet too." He gently took each one in His hands, His precious, scarred hands.

My mind flashed to Peter, and I understood a bit why he had resisted his master's touch. So vulnerable, so intimate was His touch.

"I came to serve. Not to be served. I must wash your feet, so that you will be clean all over."

My toes tickled as He wiped off the last of the muck.

As He finished, I realized the grime of my journey that had weighed me down was gone. I felt light-footed, like I could run and dance for the first time in forever.

Purity

"My Bride, I need to replace your undergarments with new ones."

With me blushing, He continued. "This gift speaks of the purity that I have given you. You have been washed completely. You are pure now."

He glanced at me, as if to ask my permission to go further. "The undergarments also speak of an intimacy that I want to have with you. Not sexual intimacy like you have with your husband, but heart intimacy that goes beyond anything in the physical. It's oneness, but in a different way."

As I opened the rectangular box lined with tissue, I lifted the delicate, lacy white garments out. "They are beautiful! Thank you," I exclaimed. I was surprised that just looking at them made me feel womanly, pretty, pure, valued. Those feelings were new to me.

The Dressing Room

"Daughter, behind you is the dressing room. It's time to get dressed now with the new garments."

As I looked back over my shoulder, a dressing room appeared with an angelic assistant holding open a purple, silken curtain. He motioned me to come. Another handed me the wedding dress, as well as a small bag with hosiery and the veil inside.

As I put on each piece, excitement welled in my chest like a bubble ready to burst. "How can this be?" I pondered in amazement. "Me? He chose me?" I looked at the dress hanging by a hook on the wall. "That dress is for me." Tears pricked my eyes. "I just can't believe it."

I held the dress in my hands before slipping it on. "It feels so pure. So holy. So unlike me." I hesitated for a moment, and then remembered my "Yes". "I can't go back on my word. Not now," I thought.

As I went through the motion of dressing myself in the wedding dress, I became aware of the prayer room again. I had moved about a quarter of the way through the labyrinth. The acceptance of each gift thus far had moved me forward a few steps each time without me being fully aware of my surroundings. The room was still quiet. It had been about twenty minutes since I had entered the room. The vision began again.

I slipped out of the dressing room, but my awkwardness showed as I stumbled forward.

"Oh, My Love," He gasped. "You are truly lovely."

Uncomfortably, I looked down at my bare feet. He laughed. "I've not forgotten your shoes."

He handed me another box. "These may help steady you a bit. I think you'll like them."

As I felt through the tissue paper, something was smooth, hard, and cool like glass.

"Oh!" I exclaimed. "Slippers." I pulled them out further. "Glass slippers!"

I began to shake my head no again with a "This is too much!" Yet, before I could say a word, He had slipped the box out of my hands and was on His knees, caressing my foot to lift it.

"Let's see if these will do," He smiled. "Yes, a perfect fit."

Before I knew what had happened, Jesus had placed both slippers on my feet. I had never worn anything so comfortable in my life. "Maybe these were made for just me," I wondered.

More Gifts

Another angelic helper with a blue sash appeared holding two more boxes inlaid with gold, one small, and one rather large.

Inquisitively, I cocked my head to the side. "More, Lord? How could you possibly give me more?"

"Oh, my supply is endless. I am the King of Kings. You are my Bride. What gift would be too great to give you?"

"But I am so unworthy, so broken," I burst into tears.

"Oh, My Love, My Bride, you are altogether lovely to me. Will you please accept my gifts to you?" Through my tears, I saw His longing to bless me, His pain again at my possible rejection.

"I don't understand this, my Lord. It feels so overwhelming, but I will receive what you want to give me."

He skipped to the angel, who took the smaller box and placed it in my hands. Inside were the most dazzling, dainty, jeweled necklace and bracelet I had ever seen.

"Jewels for my Bride. May I help you put them on?"

"Are you sure these were meant for me?"

"Of course, My Love. I designed them especially for you. Do you like them?"

"Love them," I said as my fingers glided over them, in stunned disbelief.

"There is still one last gift." He handed me the larger box. "You may need help with this one." He motioned for the angel to come and hold the box, while I peeked in.

I gasped. "A crown? A crown for my head?" I felt woozy all of a sudden as my knees grew weak. Jesus reached to steady me with His muscular arm.

"It's OK, My Love. All my Father's children have crowns to wear. You are royalty." He grinned from ear to ear. "Yours is especially beautiful - a jewel for each fruit of the Spirit I am cultivating in your heart."

"Let me help you put it on." I bowed my head in front of Him, as He placed it on my head. "Perfect. Just perfect." He appeared completely satisfied with Himself, ecstatic with joy.

The Mirror

"Come, there is a mirror up ahead. I want to show you how gorgeous you are," but I winced at His touch for though these things were stunning on the outside, on the inside I still felt deformed and disfigured, like nothing fit right, like nothing ever would. Awkwardly, I began to limp as He took my arm to usher me towards the looking glass. Somehow wearing these things only made my deformity stand out more.

I was aware that we were about halfway through the labyrinth now. I crumbled to my knees on the cloth as the door to the prayer room opened. A woman I didn't know quietly walked past me, wrote a prayer request down, and respectfully left me in peace.

"Daughter, look into the mirror."

"I can't. I just can't, Lord. You are so good. I love the gifts, but Jesus, I can't do it."

"My Love, I would never ask something of you that you couldn't do." He took my hands and lifted me to my feet. "Why won't you look into the mirror?"

I perceived He already knew the answer. I stood there, trembling uncontrollably. "I'm afraid of what I will see. I'm afraid of me."

Immediately, I flashed back as faint image of me as a fetus in my mother's womb came into focus.

"There. I created you there," He pointed. "You were created in your mother's womb by me. I knit you together and breathed breath into your lungs because I have a beautiful purpose for your life that only you can fulfill." He took a deep breath. "Every moment written about you is already recorded on your destiny scroll. I know the enemy came to steal, kill, and destroy you, but he has not succeeded. You belong to me now. You are betrothed to me. Every good plan I have had for you from the very beginning will be fulfilled."

The scene switched, and in front of me stood a little version of me, around three-years-old. I saw Jesus standing next to the little one with His hand entwined with hers. She smiled back at me.

"You were never evil, little one."

It was as if He spoke to the grown up me and the little me at the same time. I could see flashes of the tortuous abuse I had grown up with, but it was distant.

"I was always with you. You never suffered alone. And when the abuse happened, I held you right here in my arms, safe. It was never my will for you to suffer, but men have free will. Some men are deceived and obey the enemy, becoming evil and depraved. But I always held you and protected this inner part of you with me, until you were grown up and safe."

He turned to the little me. "It's time to play now."

We turned around, and as we did this beautiful garden appeared. Somehow, I knew the garden was somewhere inside of me. I was the little girl spinning around giggling as Jesus twirled her in a field of flowers.

"You are not broken. You are not deformed. You are not evil. You never were. You never will be. Please, My Love, please look in the mirror now, and see who you are created to be."

Still, I hesitated with one hand over my eyes. Cautiously, I peeked through my fingers, still half expecting to see some deformed, ugly, untouchable monster, but instead I saw me as a graceful woman with fire in my eyes - the fire of holy love. I saw beauty. Stunned, I turned to look at Jesus, but before I could say a word, He swept me up into a holy embrace. I sobbed into His shoulder. He wept with me. Then, He wiped the tears from my eyes.

The Vase

Next, He pulled out from behind His back a diamond vase that was made of small, broken pieces of glass fused together.

As He placed it in my hands, I again argued. "Oh, what if I drop it? It's so fragile."

"Actually, My Beloved, when I put together brokenness, it is indestructible. You can't break this. This was made from all the broken pieces you have given me. I have fused them back together, and now this vase is what holds all of your tears; each drop, precious to me, held in this vase in heaven until all things are redeemed."

I blinked my eyes open, waiting as they adjusted to the artificial light of the prayer room. Glancing at the clock on the wall, I muttered, "An hour has passed, but it feels like an eternity. Surely, people will start to come in soon," I thought. "Well, He's protected this time so far." I smiled to myself, "But no one will believe this."

Jesus turned to face me and gently placed my hands in His. The fire in His eyes burned clear and true.

"This, My Beloved, this place of intimacy is where you fight from. This is the place you live from. You are hidden in my love for you. Here, the enemy cannot touch you."

He stopped as if waiting for something. Then He stared straight into my eyes again as if peering into the deepest portals of my soul. "My love, there is no evil in you. There is no evil in you." I turned my head away.

"Do you not yet believe me?" I turned slowly back to meet His irresistible eyes. "Daughter, there truly is no evil in you. I have redeemed you. Called you by my name. You are mine. Where there once was darkness, there is now light – a lot of light. When the light fills you, the darkness must flee."

"There is one more thing I need to show you."

I flashed back to the day of my wedding to my earthly husband. I saw myself at the end of the day, as we were getting ready to leave the celebration. I had slipped out of my wedding gown into a more comfortable dress, but the shoes I had bought to leave in were a size too big and the bottom of them, slick. To make things worse, the exit from the building that we had chosen had several concrete steps to run down. Unbeknown to me, the steps been covered in bird seeds from over excited children ready to pelt me and my groom as we made the mad dash to our get-away car. It was a recipe for disaster, waiting to happen.

I watched as if on a movie screen: My feet flew off the first step as my new husband tried to reach for me, but it was too late. Three flights of steps I sailed down, before landing hard at an angle on my right foot.

All the emotions flooded me again like a tidal wave - humiliation, brokenness, embarrassment, anger, and fear.

Pain shot up my leg from my throbbing foot. Immediately, I knew it was broken. I had broken my foot on our wedding day.

"Why are you showing this to me now?" Hot tears filled my eyes.

"Because there is something here that I need to heal before we go on. Please, My Beloved, let me touch this."

"But I felt like a shattered, unacceptable gift to my husband for our wedding night."

Jesus's eyes were tear-filled too. "I know. And that wasn't the only reason, was it?"

I knew He was right. I had been hiding my past in a hundred tiny boxes inside, because each had been too overwhelming for me to face.

"This, My Beloved One, is what I need you to know. I never desired any of this to happen to you, not the fall, not the broken foot, but more than that not the things that shattered your heart that you kept hidden so well. I am so very sorry that those things happened to you, but that is not who I created you to be. As we become one, I will fill every broken place with my endless love. My Precious One, I have come to heal the broken hearted, to set at liberty those crushed by calamity." His tone now took on vibrant triumphant! "What was once broken, is now made whole. Where you were once filled with shame, you are now filled with grace. Where there was once terror, now peace."

"Jesus, you never lie, so this must be true, but please help me to believe you, for I feel weak."

Walking the Aisle

He offered His strong arm. "Time to walk the aisle with me." His face beamed with light, as He looped His arm in with mine. Strength shot through me. Then something began to bubble up in my belly. Joy? I hadn't remembered ever feeling that before.

"My Bride, arm in arm with me by your side, you will never stumble and fall again. Remember, this is where you fight from. This is how you win. Arm in arm with me, in intimacy with me, your Bridegroom."

A couple of others entered the prayer room and began their journey behind me. "I wonder if anyone else will experience what I have?" Yet I was too caught up in the enraptured moment to really care.

I closed my eyes as the vision came into focus again.

Lining the aisle on each side were angels of various sizes and positions all standing at attention with looks of wonder on their faces. Directly in front of us, a canopy had been erected. The aromas of honey, roses, and lilies intoxicated me. I tried to keep my wobbly steps in rhythm with His, so He held my arm steady as we approached.

Entwined in verdant vines and fragrant flowers, the canopy was breathtaking.

"My banner over you is love."

As we stepped beneath it, the Heavenly Father positioned Himself to officiate as the Holy Spirit came up beside Him.

The Father smiled at Jesus. "The time has finally come, My Son. Your bride is ready."

All heaven held its breath, as Jesus began His vows.

"My Beloved Bride, I have longed for this day to come." He choked up as He continued. "I promise you. I will never leave you nor forsake you. My love for you is stronger than death. I will never stop loving you. Nothing can separate you from my love."

Both of my hands were held securely in His. What compassion crashed over me, billowing waves of love over and over.

"Everything I have belongs to you now, all I am is yours. Just as My Father, the Spirit, and I are one, so you now are one with me. Me in you. You in me. We are completely knitted together, forever entwined as one in the bonds of love."

The Father turned to me, "And now your vows, My Daughter."

My heart seemed to pound out of my chest, but I felt the strength still coming from His being through my hands.

"Jesus, I promise to always respond to this amazing love you have for me. It is so overwhelming and hard to understand, but my answer will always be 'Yes!' to your love, 'Yes!' to you. I surrender my life to you. Everything I am and all I have belongs to you now. I love you with all my heart, my soul, and strength - with everything in me. I hold nothing back from you."

With great joy, the Father and Holy Spirit said, "Will you take each other, then?"

We both said, "I do!" in unison. A great shout of rejoicing filled the air.

He lifted my veil and gently kissed me. Electricity zinged through my body with the fire of holy love.

I stood there for what seemed like eternity enraptured by His great love as I feasted at His banqueting table.

Suiting Up

"I must prepare you for what is to come, My Bride." His tone rang with the authority of the great Warrior/King. He grinned. "You are my Warrior Bride now. You get to trample down the gates of hell with me. We will war against the great dragon together, but you must be prepared for battle."

He clapped His hands again and more angelic assistants appeared, this time holding armor. I wish I could describe to you the glory and purity that radiated from each piece. It was made from sparkling, brilliant light, yet was impenetrable.

I smoothed out my dress and sighed as I began to remove my bracelet.

"Oh no, My Darling. You get to keep all that on. That is who you are now, and remember this place of intimacy with me is where we fight from, resting in my immense love for you," He seemed giddy. "All this armor fits right over your wedding attire."

Each angel stepped forward and in turn presented their piece.

The breastplate of righteousness was brilliant with a cross mark dividing it into four sections. "Your heart is covered by my righteousness. You are forever in right standing with me."

The Bridegroom fixed securely the belt of truth around my waist. "I am the Way, the Truth, the Life. Let truth in love always be buckled around you for it will hold everything else in place."

The next angel held up my combat boots. "Must I take off these beautiful slippers?" I leaned over grabbing the heels, but Jesus gently stopped me.

"No, My Love, these boots slip on right over your slippers. There is no need to remove them. I don't take back the gifts I give, and every good gift is ultimately from my Father." He continued. "These boots though will help protect your feet and the slippers. How beautiful are the feet of them who bring good news. You will be carrying the good news of the kingdom now." So, He helped slip on the boots.

The helmet was the same. It fit perfectly with the crown, interlocking with it, yet protecting all that the crown represented of my identity in Him, as His bride. "Salvation is from me only. This helmet will protect your mind from attacks, for you are already brought to safety and salvation in me."

The shield lay on the ground next to Jesus. "The shield you must pick up, for it is your faith in me. I have given you the shield, but you are the one who must pick it up and use it." It looked heavy, but when I picked it up, it was easy to hold, and like a flash of lightning became like a force field around me.

Finally, He pulled out the sword. I have never seen anything like it before. It was brilliant as well, golden and studded with gems on the hilt. He said, "Here, for you," as He placed it in my hand. "Turn it from side to side."

As I did, I saw the word "praise" appear engraved in the sheen of the metal. Then I turned it over in my hand, and it said "Word of God". I flipped it back over, and it read "intercession". I stared at it in wonder.

Walking Out

Then, He took me by the hand and led me to the middle of the labyrinth.

Immediately, I saw the great, royal Lion of the Tribe of Judah roaring to my right. I should have been terrified, but I wasn't. Unafraid, I saw myself as a little girl, hugging tightly to the lion's neck, burying my face in its mane. Its fur was warm, light-filled, and it tickled my nose. He licked my forehead with His great tongue and nuzzled my neck in return.

Then to the right of the circle, a great, white snowy owl stood with its wings majestically tucked to its side. I trembled as I moved towards it, but from behind me, I heard the Lord say, "Look into its eyes, so you'll know it's from me."

When my courage raised enough to glance, I saw fire and wisdom in its eyes.

"This is your companion. She is white and pure, full of wisdom and fire. She is swift and insightful. She fiercely protects her young. She flies day or night. She can pierce the deepest darkness," He said. "You will need to be able to do both." He pointed to her wings, as He finished. "She can fly as high as eagles and uses the eagle's nest to care for her young. Yet, she can swoop low to attack her prey. This is your gift from my presence for this time."

I didn't know what to say, or how to thank Him, so I just turned and embraced the one to whom my heart belongs. I didn't want to let Him go.

"It's time to go now." He took my hand as we walked out of the labyrinth together.

"From this place of intimacy, we will walk this out together, arm in arm, with my authority, because it all belongs to you. You have my name now. All my authority is given to you, because you are married to me. Everything I have is yours. Everything you have is mine. You are mine and belong to me. Dream with me now!"

May the truths that He spoke on this bridal journey never fade as the Bride arises to take her place next to her valiant, glorious Bridegroom.

That concludes the vision portion of the book. In the next section, I offer some explanations of the backstory and context for different aspects of the vision. Then, there is a section for you to encounter the Bridegroom for yourself regarding the concepts in the vision. Finally, we will explore each section of the vision in more depth. Let's go on an adventure together as we further discover the preparation of the Bride of Christ.

THE BRIDAL BACKSTORY

Who is the Bride?

"Let us rejoice and exult and give him the glory,

for the marriage of the Lamb has come, and his Bride has made

herself ready; it was granted her to clothe herself with fine linen,

bright and pure"— for the fine linen is the righteous deeds of the

saints. Rev. 19:7,8 ESV

"Then one of the seven angels who had the seven bowls full of the

last seven plagues came to me and said, "Come. I will show you

the beautiful bride, the wife of the Lamb." Rev. 21:9 TPT

"He is the Bridegroom, and the bride belongs to him. I am the friend of the Bridegroom who stands nearby and listens with great joy to the Bridegroom's voice. Because of his words, my joy is complete and overflows!" John 3:29 TPT

"Husbands, love your wives [seek the highest good for her and surround her with a caring, unselfish love], just as Christ also loved the church and gave Himself up for her, so that He might sanctify the church, having cleansed her by the washing of water with the word [of God], so that [in turn] He might present the church to Himself in glorious splendor, without spot or wrinkle or any such thing; but that she would be holy [set apart for God] and blameless. Even so husbands should and are morally obligated to love their own wives as [being in a sense] their own bodies. He who loves his own wife loves himself. For no one ever hated his own body, but [instead] he nourishes and protects and cherishes it, just as Christ does the church, because we are members (parts) of His body. For this reason, a man shall leave his father and his mother and shall be joined [and be faithfully devoted] to his wife, and the two shall become one flesh. This mystery [of two becoming one] is great; but I am speaking with reference to [the relationship of] Christ and the church." Eph. 5:25-32 AMP

Some people feel that the Bible is figuratively

speaking of Jerusalem coming down from heaven as the Bride of Christ. Others feel that the Church as a whole is the Bride of Christ. Still others see it as a picture of us individually becoming one with Jesus in a holy way.

For me, my goal in writing this is not to argue my theological position nor to change anyone else's. It is to present "the mystery" in maybe a bit of a different way. God is multi-dimensional, and when He shows us images, pictures, and visions of things oftentimes they have multiple applications and layers of meaning like treasures waiting to be explored. Paul called this "a mystery" - a mystery of the two becoming one (us and Christ), which may be corporately or individually applied. I believe it is both.

Recently, at an event, during worship the leader began to spontaneously sing "Come to the wedding banquet of the Lamb." Then, we were all encouraged to imagine what that would be like. As different people (both male and female) shared their experiences, some saw the Bride of Christ as the church being married to Christ, which is a cooperate representation of the wedding of the Lamb. Others saw themselves as the Bride of Christ, in intimate fellowship and unity with Jesus. Some of the men imagined themselves dressed in wedding attire, and knew they were a part of the Bride, yet it was not a feminine expression of that, rather a perception of intimacy between Christ and them. I experienced both. I saw myself as the Bride dancing with Jesus at the wedding feast, but I also saw the Bride of Christ walking through a throng of people to meet the Bridegroom. Whether you are male or female, I encourage you to receive from this imagery in whatever way the Lord leads.

In Revelation 21, the Bride of Christ is portrayed as the New Jerusalem coming down to marry Jesus Christ. This is also a corporate form of being the Bride. As children of God, we are a part of the New Jerusalem.

What an amazing, beautiful experience is awaiting us in the marriage of the Lamb!

Leading Up To

Years before this experience that I just wrote about happened, I had embarked on an inner healing journey when my former pastor suggested that I needed some help. Even though I had been raised in the church, gone to Bible college, married "Mr. Right", had three beautiful children, and did all the "right" things as a "Christian", I deeply struggled with depression, anxiety, and panic attacks.

From all outside views, I had a great life, but inwardly, I was a train wreck. For many years, I didn't know why. My inner healing journey began a process of uncovering unprocessed pain in my heart, surrendering the pain to Jesus, Him speaking truth to me on many levels, and then me walking into more freedom and healing in Him.

Some experience instantaneous deliverance and healing. I've had those beautiful moments of God encounters where I was instantly delivered and healed, but more often, I've walked through a tedious, uphill journey of process. Most of us don't like the slow-cooker seasons in life, but God is developing flavor in us, called the fruit of the Spirit, when we yield to the process.

Up to this point, lots of changes had occurred on our church front. After having just come out of a painful church split, I found myself offering a hesitant "yes" to attending this women's retreat.

Because of a previous vow of "I'll never do THAT again", it was my first reattempt at coming to a women's retreat in years.

Nevertheless, I joined these women on a Georgia mountain, mostly ladies I didn't know. I came to it heavy - like with bricks on my shoulders — heavy-laden with responsibility, with sorrow, with haunting pieces. I came with a desperate feeling of being overwhelmed, like I wasn't enough for the things the Lord was asking of me. I came fearful of exposure, of being rejected, and of being tossed away if anyone really knew me and what my past had held.

Yet, I knew I was in preparation mode for things the Lord was moving me towards - some shifts and changes in me, in ministry, and for a major prayer assignment I felt completely ill-equipped to carry out. I longed for my heart to be settled and prepared for what was ahead.

At the retreat, friends had painstakingly prepared a prayer room for the women to meet with the Lord in prayer and meditation. The leader had gone to another ministry to borrow a hand-painted cloth with a detailed labyrinth meticulously crafted on it. This filled the floor of the prayer room.

Labyrinths

There are different types of labyrinths throughout history that date back as far as Ancient Egypt and Greek mythology. Some are mazes (which is not the kind I am referring to), and some are forward pathways that are primarily used as tools of prayer and meditation, particularly by early Christians, to process out a journey with the Lord in a methodical, meditative manner.

Early on, they were used in church history as a substitute for a pilgrimage to Jerusalem. Then later, they more commonly were walked upon to process out life's issues, like grief, in a prayerful release to God.

Many times, they are found in gardens near churches with the pathway hedged in by foliage. They are created in a circular path that weaves back and forth until it converges in the center circle. The one at this retreat was simply painted on a piece of cloth, so that it could be moved from event to event. It is not the cloth or the labyrinth that created the atmosphere for meeting with the Lord. The prayers of those who prepared the room ushered the presence of God in. The labyrinth is simply a tool, to provide a place - a method to meet with God.

One thing that struck me when studying the history of labyrinths is that it represents a journey. It is not a maze meant to trap or confuse you. It is a forward moving pathway that portrays process with God, relationship with God. In fact, in Jewish weddings the bride circles the groom seven times before meeting him in the middle under the wedding canopy. The labyrinth I walked on that day had seven layers or rings that went around the center, so literally it was if I was circling the center where I met Jesus under the chuppah. How awesome is it that God chose this way of meeting with me to represent the relational process of the preparation of the Bride of Christ!

Visions and Seeing in the Spirit

We experience God through many ways: reading the Holy Bible, listening to teachers, through prayer, nature, other people, through the quiet voice of the Holy Spirit within us, through dreams, and visions, music, etc.

*"And it shall come to pass afterward, that I will pour out my Spirit on all flesh; your sons and your daughters shall prophesy, your old men shall **dream dreams**, your young men shall have visions." Joel 2:28 ESV*

God loves us and desires to talk to us, to communicate with us. He wants us to know Him. So, I believe He is always trying to speak to us in ways that we can receive Him.

Our mind's eye or imagination screen is one way that the Lord wants to engage with us.

There are different types of dreams and visions. The kind that this experience was is what I would call an open vision.

I first began seeing images of Jesus in my inner healing experiences. With a healing prayer minister present, we would ask Jesus to show me the root of whatever pain I was experiencing. As Jesus would open up those very painful memories, I would ask the true Lord Jesus to come into the memory, into the pain with me, and He would. I would see a visual image in my mind's eye of His presence. He showed me the truth about the situations, and as I forgave and released what had happened, He took the pain away.

It was in these very hurtful memories that I first began to really experience the depth of who Jesus is. As I've continued the journey of encountering Him, He keeps expanding that ability to hear Him, see Him, and know Him. Now, as I see Him with me, I don't always have something painful to look at. Most of the time, He just may have something He wants to talk to me about or show me. I believe for all eternity we will be discovering new, wonderful things about God, because He is infinite and eternal.

Many times, for me seeing visions is more like an impression, where I just know what I'm seeing. After the fact, that impression becomes clearer and clearer, like the opposite of a dream. I'm not perfect in this, nor do I always perceive everything well. I just desire to be a friend of Jesus. I desire to know Him more than anything, the real Him.

"For now we see in a mirror dimly, but then face- to-face. Now I know in part; then I shall know fully, even as I have been fully known." 1 Cor. 13:12 ESV

My biggest rule of thumb is this. Does what I'm perceiving line up with who God is revealed through His written word? Does it line up with His character and nature as revealed in the Holy Bible?

Open visions are like pictures or movies that run on your imagination screen – in your mind's eye. You can tell that you are still present in reality, yet you are experiencing something or are somewhere else at the same time. There are times it can be so real that it seems you are actually there, with your senses fully engaged, but other times it is more like a movie screen in front of you that the vision runs on.

This open vision was more like the full-immersion kind. Imagine going on a ride at theme park where you know you are sitting in a chair, yet it feels like you just took flight into another world. You aren't really moving. If you looked down you could see your feet solid on the ground, but the large screen in front of you and the sounds you are hearing make you feel like you are somewhere else.

The Struggle for Men

Men often struggle to understand how they can be considered a part of "the Bride of Christ". It can appear weird and confusing imagery.

Rather than me trying to explain this, the following heavenly encounter is one that Christopher Carter wrote about in his book, "In the Palace of Heaven". This is an excerpt from chapter six entitled, "The King's Bedchamber". Since Christopher is definitely a man, I appreciate his willingness to allow me to share with you his encounter with the Lord.

"…As Jesus was walking me through the crowd (in the heavenly throne room), He directed me down a hallway away from the grand room and all the activity. We arrived at a set of blue and gold doors, just as massive and ornate as the ones at the entrance and walked into a much quieter environment. The room was smaller and richly decorated, but there were no angels hustling around doing their work. It was just me and Jesus, and that made it a lot easier to take it all in."

"It was a bedroom, and it was extravagant. Everything looked gilded with gold, from the furniture to the designs in the ceiling and even the floor. Everywhere I looked, I saw only the finest materials, and over the bed was a canopy of rich blues, purples, and reds. It was the bedchamber of a King. Jesus had spent those moments silently watching me roam about the room in awe. He wore His usual smile, like He always does when He knows He's showing me something that makes my jaw drop. Then, He walked over to the bed and sat down on it, and then invited me to do the same. That's when it hit me. This was a bedroom. I was in Jesus's bedroom."

"Suddenly, I had a sense of Jesus being the Bridegroom, and I, as a believer, being His Bride (Ephesians 5:22-33). I admit that felt a little awkward at first. I'm a married man, and I like being masculine, so understanding my relationship to Him, as the Bride didn't feel immediately natural. He gave me the "don't worry" look and invited me again to sit on the bed with Him. As I did, the colorful fabric canopies dropped down to completely enclose the bed. We sat there in total privacy. Then, with His usual grin, Jesus said, "Christopher, don't think of marriage in terms of gender, think in terms of covenant." Those explanations certainly made me feel better. It wasn't an affront to my masculinity to sit on this bed with Him because He was making a greater point about what marriage means in the context of God and man. We know what marriage is between a man and a woman on earth, but it also applies to Jesus and His Bride – His Church. But it stretches our brains a little to think of marriage on those terms, unless we understand it as a very specific kind of relationship with unequaled privileges. So, what does it mean to be married to God (especially if you're a man)? These are my thoughts:

- In marriage you share everything
- In marriage you know each other intimately
- The marriage relationship is different from every other relationship in life. It's the only one that enjoys those privileges above.

Jesus looked at me over His brow and said, 'Christopher, that's what I want with you. I want to share everything I have with you. I want us to know each other intimately, and I want this relationship and its privileges to be special.'

That kind of unity is hard enough to understand (and achieve) with an earthly spouse; but it's exactly what the Lord wants between us with Him…"

Understanding Intimacy Versus Sex

Many times, people only equate intimacy with sex, and the consummation of marriage in the natural is sexual intimacy. In regard to our relationship with Jesus being the Bridegroom or our husband, we can struggle with this imagery, especially in our over sexualized culture, but even more so for sexual abuse survivors. I know personally I've had a very hard time separating out in my mind's eye the idea of intimacy and sex.

I want to be very clear. When I'm talking about intimacy with Jesus or with God, it is not about sexual relationship at all. Jesus is God. He is not sexual, because He is not a man. He came as a man, yes, but He is now glorified. Even though He still has the appearance of a man, He has no desire towards us sexually.

The intimacy that Jesus and indeed the family (Father, Son, and Holy Spirit) want to have with us is a holy oneness that far exceeds any oneness achieved in sexual intimacy.

This quote from Pam VandenBulck with "Oaks Rising" further explains this.

"God is love. We have established that love is something that is a relational connection of intimacy that is equal. I want to know you, and you want to know me. So together we come in intimacy saying *into me you see*, so it's an opening up of my heart to that person. When I open up my heart, I create an environment of intimacy to be known. I open up the door, and say you can come in, and you can know me. I'm willing to take down the façades and masks. So, that's intimacy. It is a relational connection that has nothing to do with sex."

Wake Up!

"' After this I let my devotion slumber, but my heart for him stayed awake. I had a dream. I dreamed of my beloved — he was coming to me in the darkness of night. The melody of the man I love awakened me. I heard his knock at my heart's door as he pleaded with me.'

The Bridegroom-King - 'Arise, my love. Open your heart, my darling, deeper still to me. Will you receive me this dark night? There is no one else but you, my friend, my equal. I need you this night to arise and come be with me. You are my pure, loyal dove, a perfect partner for me. My flawless one, will you arise? For my heaviness and tears are more than I can bear. I have spent myself for you throughout the dark night.' "

Song of Songs 5:2 TPT

"Awake, O sleeper, and arise from the dead, and Christ will shine on you." Eph. 5:14 ESV

Several years ago, my husband and I escaped for an anniversary weekend away to revisit where we had gone on our honeymoon. The morning sunlight gently peeked through the curtains of our hotel room and cast a slender beam across our bed. Heavily, my husband grunted and turned to face me. "I had the weirdest dream." After a long pause and a diverted look of shame across his face, I prodded him to tell me the dream, assuring him I wouldn't overreact.

"Well, I dreamt I was asleep in bed and suddenly woke up, but there was another woman lying next to me." He shifted his weight around, while his leg began to nervously shake. "I don't understand. I've not been thinking about any other women. I only want to be with you. In my dream, I was shocked that I was in bed with someone else, but I was sleepy and foggy headed, and it was taking a while to wake up, to get out of bed."

Normally, in a situation like this, hearing such a dream would have sent me into a downward spiral of feelings of betrayal and being an insufficient bride. My husband knew that.

Yet instead, there was an inner knowing that my husband's dream meant something more. I calmly looked him in the eyes to reassure him he wasn't in for a hurricane of emotions. "I think I know what your dream means."

"You do?" he stuttered. "But I promise that I…"

"It wasn't about you, honey. In fact, you were representing the Bride of Christ."

"But I…" I continued past his look of confusion.

"The church, the Bride of Christ has been asleep with other lovers without even knowing it. But she is waking up to find the state she has been in. She is still sleepy though and groggy, but she is waking up, and is ready to throw off the covers, repent for her actions, and be made ready for her true Beloved."

We both sat stunned, but it resonated in me as if someone had just hit a gong. Since that time, there has been a shift that has been like a very slow waking up process for the Bride of Christ – a realization of sleeping with other lovers, and with that, an acceptance of that invitation of Jesus to get out of bed, repent, and make preparations.

The Bride Arising is both a corporate and individual "becoming" or "realization" of who Jesus has called us to be, but we each have a choice whether we will wake up, get out of bed, and come meet with Him when He calls. We have to leave the other lovers, which may be things, people, or systems that we have put before Him - the things we have taken comfort in, rather than Him.

It feels vulnerable and a bit risky to step out of our comfort zone into a new place with Him, and there will be some cleaning up, restoration that needs to happen, but this is what He is calling us into so that we will be ready for our groom.

"For your Maker is your husband, the Lord of hosts is his name; and the Holy One of Israel is your Redeemer, the God of the whole earth he is called. For the Lord has called you like a wife deserted and grieved in spirit, like a wife of youth when she is cast off, says your God. For a brief moment I deserted you, but with great compassion I will gather you. In overflowing anger for a moment, I hid my face from you, but with everlasting love I will have compassion on you," says the Lord, your Redeemer.

Isaiah 54:5-8 ESV

"The season has changed, the bondage of your barren winter has ended, and the season of hiding is over and gone. The rains have soaked the earth and left it bright with blossoming flowers. The

season for singing and pruning the vines has arrived. I hear the cooing of doves in our land, filling the air with songs to awaken you and guide you forth. Can you not discern this new day of destiny breaking forth around you? The early signs of my purposes and plans are bursting forth. The budding vines of new life are now blooming everywhere. The fragrance of their flowers whisper, 'There is change in the air.' Arise, my love, my beautiful companion, and run with me to the higher place. For now is the time to arise and come away with me."

Song of Songs 2:11-13 TPT

ENCOUNTERING THE BRIDEGROOM

Let's take a few minutes to talk about what it

looks like for you to also walk into this place of intimacy
with your Savior, the True Lord Jesus. As I said in the
introduction, this is not a to do list of requirements that
you do to be prepared. This is about a relationship,
where Jesus walks you through finding out your own
identity in Him. I hope that as you read the vision, you
could see Jesus preparing you as well.

As I spend time in the Word of God and in
meditative prayer, I listen with my spiritual inner ear to

hear God's voice speaking to me about the things He is showing me. Other times, I will ask part of the Trinity to show me a safe place where I can meet with Him in my inner self.

A great way to start that process is to simply sit in a chair and visualize the room around you with your eyes closed. As you do this, ask Jesus (or Holy Spirit or Papa God) to help you to see where He is with you. If you could see Jesus in the room with you, where would He be and what would He look like? Then just simply ask Him what He wants you to know, what does He want to be for you right now, or is there something He wants to show you about who He has created you to be. There can be a number of questions like this that you may ask Him. Think about what you might talk with your best friend about.

For example, I've been in the middle of a room with hundreds of people, and all of a sudden felt overwhelmed and anxious. When I stopped on the inside to ask Jesus to show me where He was right then in that room with me, and then asked Him what He wanted me to know, He instantly showed me. His peaceful presence overtook me, bringing me the truth. All the anxiety left. All I did was remember to ask Him. I just took that second to engage His presence which was already there.

He is so present with us and wants us to walk with Him as a friend, throughout our day. Many times, we just aren't aware of where He is or what He is doing in our day to day. Taking time to meditate on Him, and what He wants us to know, helps us to walk in His presence and truth. It helps us to develop that trust and intimacy, which is foundational.

Find a quiet, a safe spot, and just focus on God. Ask Him what part of the Trinity would He want you to engage with, and let's spend some time exploring this bridal journey with Him.

Make sure that this feels safe, feels like love. I love to look in Jesus's eyes, and see His great compassion for me. Look for the scars in His hands and feet. That is proof you are sensing the correct one.

Remember anything the Lord says will always line up to the Holy Bible, and His character and nature revealed in the Holy Bible. He is good. He is love.

Everything you experience should line up to those two very important principles. If you hear or sense something that is evil, shameful, or not in agreement with God's word like "Go steal a piece of gum," then it's not God. God will convict us of things in us at times that need to change, but He doesn't condemn us. Jesus said that He didn't come to condemn the world, but that the world might be saved through Him. That's in John 3:17.

If you don't sense anything, you may need a little help from a trusted friend or counselor to feel safe. Trust is the biggest key to engaging with God.

As we go through each stage, I encourage you to pray, asking the Lord these questions or questions of your own, and record His answers in the space provided. If you feel comfortable, allow Him to minister to you however He chooses. That may include showing you a safe place in your mind's eye for you to meet. If you find that you get triggered into negative emotions or behavior, you may need to stop and seek help from a trusted friend or counselor who can walk beside you during this process. I've included prayers, but please feel free to use your own instead. This is your relationship with God.

The Prayer Encounter:

(Whatever Person of the Trinity you are meeting with), I accept your invitation to come and meet with you today. I know you are already in me and desire for me to know my Bridegroom more fully. Thank you that you are in me, and I'm in you. Thank you that we are one in Jesus. Because you are in me, I can hear and perceive you. Thank you for this, _____.

I receive all that Jesus has done for me in purchasing this marriage covenant through His perfect work at the cross. I ask that my spiritual ears would be open to hear you now, my spiritual eyes be open to see and perceive you now, that my heart will know you, sense you, feel your presence in me. If there is anything blocking this from happening in me or around me, please clear the way for me to only receive from you now through my savior, the true Lord Jesus Christ and His finished work on the cross.

Lord, I ask you to show me whatever you want me to see and tell me whatever you want me to know. I yield to you now.

In Jesus' name

As you spend time with the Lord, ask Him to show you where He is around you right now. Once you perceive Him, ask Him if He wants to come closer to you, or does He want you to come closer to Him? Just let that happen.

Here are some questions based on the vision for you to ask Him regarding your own journey. Please feel free to engage with God however He wants you to. He loves you, and He always honors our free will.

_____, *am I still holding on to or wearing any old garments that I need to give to you? If so, I choose to give these to you now. I say yes and receive the new wedding gown, garment of salvation, and robe of righteousness you want to give me. Would you please show that to me now?* See yourself wrapped in the robe of righteousness. What does your wedding garment look like?

_____

_____

_____

_____

_____

Is there something that you want me to give you in our wedding gift exchange? What do you want to give me, Lord? Do that exchange with your Bridegroom.

_____

_____

_____

_____

_____

What areas of me do you still need to clean up, Lord? Would you bathe them now and cleanse them with the holy water of the Holy Spirit? See God cleansing any part of you that needs cleaning.

_____

_____

_____

_____

_____

_____, *are there any areas of me*
- in my mind, soul, spirit, or body - where I still feel impure or I
struggle to see it as pure and clean through your precious blood?
Is there any area where I am holding onto something impure,
like unforgiveness, a lie, an unholy judgment, vow, or sinful
behavior? If so, I place that into the cross now. I ask you to
forgive me, and I choose to forgive and to release to you (the
person's name).

I place them into your hands for you to do whatever you
deem best with them or that situation. I receive your purity into
every part of my spirit, soul, and body now. (This is almost
always a process, and you may come back to several times.)
Thank you for your forgiveness. See those areas as pure
now. Watch what God does as He shows you what that
purity looks like.

_____

_____

_____

_____

_____

_____, *may I enter the dressing room now, and place on the wedding attire you have provided for me?* As He says yes, notice each piece of the wedding attire He is giving you, and what they represent. See yourself putting on each piece with thankfulness.

_____

_____

_____

_____

_____

Lord, are there any other wedding gifts you wish to give me? As you receive what He has, note if any have a special meaning to you personally. Let Him lavish you with His love for you. Spend time thanking Him as you receive the wonderful gifts that He has saved just for you.

_____

_____

_____

_____

_____

_____, *is it time to look in the mirror?* (If at any time, God says He wants to do something different than what we are praying, I would encourage you to let Him.) Let God give you the mirror. This part is all about your identity and seeing yourself the way God has truly made you to be. If there is any part of this that makes you uncomfortable, ask the Lord to show you any lie-based thinking regarding your identity, and ask Him to tell you the truth about who He created you to be.

As you look in the mirror, and see who you really are in Him, receive that holy, good image. If there is anything about that image that is not good, go back and ask Him more questions regarding it. Let Him continue to show you where any false identity may be coming from, and let Him heal those areas. (Again, this may take some time.) In the end, the image you should see of yourself will be the God-given image and identity that He created you to be from the foundation of the world, and it is VERY GOOD.

_____, *are there any tears from mourning or grieving that you need me to place in my vase? May I see my vase? How do you see my vase, my pain, my tears, and my grief? I release my grief and tears to you. Thank you for giving me a garment of praise instead a heavy spirit.* Watch the Lord, and see what He does here. Thank Him for removing any veils of sorrow or mourning, and watch Him place the garment of praise on you instead.

_____

_____

_____

_____

_____

Lord, is it time to walk the aisle now? If it is, see Him and yourself walking the aisle and meeting Holy Spirit and Papa God at the end of the aisle. Notice the Chuppah of Love (His banner over you is love) that you stand under. (It might be good to write out your vows below, just to remember.) Allow Jesus to say His vows to you, and then you say your vows to Him.

_____, *will you give me my*

armor now? As He gives it to you, notice each piece, and anything that is unique about it to you. How is it made uniquely for you?

Helmet of Salvation -

_____

_____

Breastplate of Righteousness -

_____

_____

Belt of Truth -

_____

_____

Shoes of Peace -

_____

_____

Shield of Faith -

_____

_____

Sword of the Spirit -

_____

_____

Any other pieces of armor just for me -

_____

_____, *is there anything else you want to say or do for me during this time together?* Just receive whatever else He wants to tell you or show you as you finish your time with Him. Thank Him for all He has done!

_____

_____

_____

_____

_____

_____, I ask you to seal everything you just did for me and said to me by the power of the Holy Spirit. Thank you for being my Bridegroom and preparing me more as your Bride. I say, "Come, Lord Jesus."

Through the rest of the book, I will go back and explore each part of the vision from my own point of view. I will refer to some things in my own healing journey, but I am not a therapist or a licensed counselor. The things I share and explain are from the standpoint of having walked through a lot of my own healing journey. Some concepts have come from multiple inner healing ministries, which I have found all hold to the same basic principles, though some terms may be different with each ministry. My sharing is not to meant to define your relationship with the Lord or to make you feel badly if your journey is different. All our stories are uniquely different, so the way God relates to us will be unique to us. I celebrate this! Hopefully, my sharing of my personal viewpoint of the journey will add more context and help you on your own journey with the Lord.

EXPLORING THE VISION

The Great Exchange

The old dress and garments represented

several things to me in this vision. Because I believe this bridal journey is for many more people than just me, those garments, as well as other things, will represent different things to you. Just like lyrics to a song may hold different feelings, memories, or represent different perceptions depending on the listener, so each scene throughout this vision may mean something different to you.

For me, the old ripped, bloody dress represented my past, the abuse that had been perpetrated on me, the aftermath of shame, fear, and anger that were still like clothing wrapped around me.

When you have worn those things for so long, you don't really understand the heaviness and burden of it all. It just becomes your normal, and oddly enough when we are offered the new, gorgeous gown, it can feel very insecure, even unbelievable.

For me, I've struggled to feel worthy, good enough to receive these things from the Lord or others. Sometimes, it feels scary to give up the old familiar patterns of thinking or habits, rather than to step into the new truth of my identity. Allowing Jesus access to those places in my heart can feel vulnerable and exposing.

To embrace the new wedding dress and allow Jesus to put it on you means accepting the new relationship that the dress represents and yielding to Jesus who is forming that new identity of who He has called you to be in Him. He already knows your whole story anyway, because He was there - He is timeless and all present. Yet, it is a different posture to allow yourself to be open, to be vulnerable, because in doing so you can open yourself up to being hurt.

To stay in the old meant you had some control, false control. You could stay sealed up, your heart impenetrable, your emotions numb. Learning to trust love is learning to allow your defenses to be lowered to allow love in.

Part of the enemy's agenda is to destroy trust in us at a very young age. The very ones we should develop trust with often break it, crushing our hearts through abuse, lies, deceit, and betrayal.

Yet the real Jesus is not like that at all.

For me, that was especially hard to understand because much of the abuse that I endured from childhood happened within the context of church. I had many false Jesus' voices that were abusive, controlling, and harmful. In that context, God was one to be feared, not loved. He was ready to strike me down, not wrap me in safe, loving arms, or so I thought. I really didn't know what the words *safe*, *trust*, and *love* meant.

The real Jesus has had to slowly and meticulously rebuild the framework of trust with me, because trusting my naked heart to Him was extremely frightening. He is faithful, gentle, and kind. Every time I've let Him in, He has always overwhelmed me with His great love for me, healing my heart more and more each time.

He is not coming as a voyeur or a harsh judge to expose our pain, shame, fears, and hatred. He is coming to blanket us in His love, building trust with us, so that we can fully receive the new gorgeous dress He purchased for us.

"To grant [consolation and joy] to those who mourn in Zion—to give them an ornament (a garland or diadem) of beauty instead of ashes, the oil of joy instead of mourning, the garment [expressive] of praise instead of a heavy, burdened, and failing spirit.." Isaiah 61:3 AMPC

The First Gift – Covenant Relationships

In most cultures, including the Hebrew culture, gifts between the bride and groom are more than just customary. They are a part of making a covenant with one another. In other words, if a groom were to offer his gift to his beloved bride, and she refused to receive the gift for whatever the reason, she is refusing him as a husband. She is refusing the marriage covenant.

At the time of my vision, I had no understanding of this, but as I later listened to two different friends explain this concept to me, Jesus's reaction in the vision now made sense.

"You don't like it? You don't accept? You don't accept Me?"

In my initial refusal of the wedding gift because of my own feelings of unworthiness and shame, I almost refused my Bridegroom.

So many times, people refuse God and His goodness because of shame, self-hatred, guilt, condemnation, unbelief, etc. They think they have to be good enough to receive the gift. Yet, no one ever will be.

The fact that Jesus chose us and is offering the gift qualifies us to receive it. When we receive the wedding gift, we receive Him, the covenant of marriage. When we receive His gift of His life given for us, the work of salvation at the cross, we receive the marriage covenant. We are saying, "Yes, I will receive you, Jesus, as the lover of my soul."

Recently, a friend asked to borrow some silver pieces I had inherited from my husband's side of the family to use for her wedding reception. The pieces were badly tarnished with years of grime built up, so I squirted silver cleaner onto a soft cloth and began to rub the layers of black tarnish off of the trays.

As the tarnish began to fade in a circle and the beautiful silver gleamed through, I began to ask myself why I had not shined them up years ago. All of a sudden, the truth hit smack in my chest. I had never felt good enough to receive them. I believed the precious things inherited from my husband's side of the family were my girls' inheritance. Not mine.

I had them in my house for years, but never took ownership of them; therefore, I never polished them and enjoyed the beauty of them, because I was just passing them down. How sad.

In that moment of staring into my reflection in the shiny silver tray, Jesus spoke to my heart, "You are worthy to receive all that I have given you. All the inheritance is yours to enjoy. You didn't do anything to earn it. You just said, 'I do.' Everything I have is yours freely given to you. You are worthy to receive it because you are my bride."

The Cleansing Water

In preparation for a traditional Jewish wedding, both the bridegroom and the bride bathe separately in what is called the "mikveh" or ritual bath. This ritual cleansing signifies the holy transition from being single to married, which represents the purification process of presenting the "spotless", pure bride and bridegroom.

Jesus also submitted himself to the ritual cleansing of baptism, performed by John, the Baptist. Can you imagine Jesus Christ as the bridegroom, preparing himself through the ritual bath for His bride, even though He was already the "spotless lamb"?

In the vision of the Bride, the washing process is possibly one of the most important steps to preparation.

Ceremonial washing was not only required, but there were hefty consequences if the process was not followed correctly, especially for the priests of the temple. If they stood before the altar unclean, they would die. It was the simple act of obedience of washing with water from the laver outside the temple, that symbolically washed away their defilement, their sin, preparing them to enter the Holy of Holies, or the Bridal Chamber – the place of face-to-face intimacy with the Lord.

Washing Feet

There is something very vulnerable about letting someone touch or wash your feet.

For the Jews, it was a necessary task done at the door of their home as they entered in. For those who were well off enough to have slaves, the job of "foot-washer" would have been considered the lowest of jobs for a slave to do. Yet, part of the reason it was so necessary was when they would eat, they would lie on the floor on mats. Can you imagine what a mess they would have with the road grime from a day of walking mingled in with their food, if they had not washed their feet? Here's one of the most precious accounts of Jesus found in scripture to me.

"Jesus, knowing that the Father had given all things into his hands, and that he had come from God and was going back to God, rose from supper. He laid aside his outer garments, and taking a towel, tied it around his waist. Then he poured water into a basin and began to wash the disciples' feet and to

wipe them with the towel that was wrapped around him. He came to Simon Peter, who said to him, "Lord, do you wash my feet?" Jesus answered him, "What I am doing you do not understand now, but afterward you will understand." Peter said to him, "You shall never wash my feet." Jesus answered him, "If I do not wash you, you have no share with me." Simon Peter said to him, "Lord, not my feet only but also my hands and my head!" Jesus said to him, "The one who has bathed does not need to wash, except for his feet, but is completely clean. And you are clean, but not every one of you."' John 13:3-10 ESV

Later, Jesus instructed His disciples to wash each other's feet. This was such an act of such humble love on both parts. To stoop down and wash someone else's feet takes some humility.

There have been a few times Jesus has had me do this for others, and honestly, I didn't want to do it. In fact, I had said to myself that I'd never wash others feet. Yet, as I stepped into obedience with two different people at separate times, it broke something off of them that had been present before. It broke something off of me too.

Everyone is precious to the Lord. Everyone. Jesus stooped to wash even the one who would betray Him, knowing all along the kiss of betrayal on His cheek was coming that very night. That's unconditional love.

I've also been on the receiving end of having my feet washed, and it feels very vulnerable. I can relate to Peter saying "no" to the Lord. For me, one reason it feels so vulnerable is that it is a love that has no bounds. God's love has no limits towards us, and there is a sense of uncontrollable-ness about it.

When someone stoops to wash your feet, they are choosing to come close enough not only to see your messiness, but to possibly get some of that dirt on them in the cleansing process. To think of Jesus as being not only willing to wash me, but to take my smelly crud on Himself, so that He would wipe it all away, feels like too much sometimes. He stoops to the lowest places, the muddy pits I've been stuck in, and He lifts me up out of them.

When Peter countered Jesus telling Him that He would not let Him wash His feet, Jesus said, "Then you can have no part of me." Why? Because Jesus is the only one who can truly wash our filth away, and if He doesn't, we can't enter the place of feasting intimately with Him. We have to be cleansed.

I've asked Jesus why He didn't want to wash all of Peter. I believe it's because the heart position of being cleansed, humbled, and receiving His work of love was enough. The other wasn't needed.

So often because of the defilement that happens in certain types of abuse, like sexual abuse, Jesus wants to cleanse or wash each area. Sometimes, we need to see Him washing our eyes of the trauma we saw, our ears of the trauma we heard, our mouth of the things that touched our lips, etc. If Jesus leads that way, it's best to follow that leading. He always knows how to heal us, and sometimes we need a good bath, a good cleansing of all the things that may have defiled us and kept us from intimacy with Him.

Rivers of Healing Waters

Recently, the Lord has given me a lot of imagery of bathing, soaking, swimming in the River of Life, and being immersed in waterfalls, so much so that Jesus often uses that imagery as He heals and washes His children clean as I engage in ministry times with others.

Many passages in scripture show water imagery. In Ezekiel 47, the River of Life flows from beneath the temple down, to the lowest places, bringing life wherever it goes. In fact, the trees that grow on the banks of the river have leaves that won't wither, nor will their fruit fail, because it is fed by the water that flows from the sanctuary.

In John 4, Jesus also explains to the woman at the well that He gives Living Water that will quench our thirst forever in Him.

"And afterwards I will pour out My Spirit upon all flesh…"
Joel 2:28 AMPCE

This speaks of the last days, when God's Spirit is poured out without measure, over the whole earth. What an amazing picture of the powerful, cleansing waters of the Holy Spirit.

As I'm writing this, I'm sitting by our pond listening to water trickle over the rocks down a small waterfall. Many times, the Lord has used water imagery with me in that idea of cleansing and being set free. His water always flows to the lowest places bringing life and refreshment to all it touches.

Sometimes, I've heard the Lord say to come sit in the healing baths, and I've seen me following Him up a spiral staircase to baths in the heavenly high places. All I know is that for me as I've pictured myself soaking in those baths, my heart has felt comforted, at peace, immersed in love.

Lately, He has called me to come higher still, and I've stood at the base of the most massive, crashing waterfalls you can imagine. As the mist of them refreshed me, I saw white eagles circling the top. I knew these waters were from the very throne of God.

There have been times Jesus has said to jump in the water. Normally, it looks like the river of life in my mind's eye. As I have seen myself jumping in, many times Jesus begins splashing with me. There is a child-like joy found playing in the water. Again, things holding me back, lies I have believed often just wash away. Often, unprompted, this type of imagery has come up with others I know as well.

Maybe you think I just have a creative imagination. Maybe? Yet often others share almost identical, healing experiences with the Lord.

We must be cleansed before we can put on the bridal clothes. Could you imagine a bride covered in grime, yet dressed in her gown? We can't step into the next phase of the bridal journey without the precious washing of Jesus.

Wash me, Lord Jesus, and I will be whiter than snow. Fill me with your living water, quenching my thirst.

Purity and The Dressing Room

In our culture, we have lost much of the honor and respect that goes along with a wedding, but not so in most cultures. It would be unthinkable for a bride not to be properly dressed for her special day. The following story emphasizes the importance of being properly dressed when invited to a wedding.

"But when the king came in to see the guests, he spotted a man who was not dressed in wedding clothes. 'Friend,' he asked, 'how did you get in here without wedding clothes?' But the man was speechless. Then the king told the servants, 'Tie him hand and foot, and throw him into the outer darkness, where there will be weeping and gnashing of teeth.' For many are called, but few are chosen." Matt. 22:11-14 ESV

Because the man refused to put on the clothes that had been provided for the wedding by the King, he was rejected from the ceremony.

Many places in the Word of God explain what our new clothes look like.

"I will greatly rejoice in the Lord; my soul shall exult in my God, for he has clothed me with the garments of salvation; he has covered me with the robe of righteousness, as a bridegroom decks himself like a priest with a beautiful headdress, and as a bride adorns herself with her jewels."
Isaiah 61:10 ESV

Righteousness is not something we do, but it is what has been done for us. Jesus purchased the robes of righteousness and the beautiful wedding dress for His Bride. It is a gift of right standing with God, of right relationship, through a marriage covenant with Jesus that grants us all the fullness of oneness with the Trinity.

The garments are handcrafted just for you - a perfect fit.

Often, I've seen images of taking off old, worn, dirty clothes, and putting on the new clothes Jesus has provided. This imagery has represented different things along my healing journey. I've seen Him do the same for many others.

Sometimes, it has represented taking off old, sinful mindsets or actions. At other times, depression or other things have weighed me down. Putting on the new garments might mean letting praise and thankfulness come out of my heart.

One of my most precious experiences of this came at a time of desperation. I was being sucked down a vortex of depression and experiencing insomnia. A dear friend called to check on me, because Jesus had given her a vision of me being cut up and wounded with deep gashes oozing blood all over a soiled, torn dress. She witnessed Jesus running up to me with bandages and healing ointment. After He healed the wounds, He offered me a new wedding gown. As she told me this story, I envisioned it and later painted it. What a beautiful exchange of giving Jesus my filthy, dirty rags and receiving His amazing dress of righteousness and relationship. (The painting of this experience is at the beginning of the vision.)

In the vision, He also gave me a new set of undergarments. This was the most difficult to take because of how vulnerable it felt. He knew all of the sexual trauma and abuse I had gone through as a child, and He was offering the gift of virginity, of a new, pure, holy start.

As I put on each piece, I felt completely safe in the changing booth He had created. I remember how terribly vulnerable and awkward I felt, but He never violated my trust in any way, while waiting patiently outside for me to fully dress. So tender is the Lord with the broken hearted. He knows the trauma we have endured, and in receiving even the undergarments it was a completely fresh, clean beginning - fully receiving the finished work He had done.

Does this mean I don't still struggle? Of course not. I still walk out my freedom journey daily. Sometimes, it is still challenging to receive this new identity, but I keep saying "yes."

From this position of who I am in Jesus, dressed in His righteousness, I've come to realize that it is a state of being. No matter what lies I still believe or pain I am still struggling with, no matter what life throws my way, the truth is that I am the beloved Bride who Jesus chose from the foundation of the world.

Of course, the shoes hinted of Cinderella. I've wondered why He used that imagery. Maybe because He is our Knight in Shining Armor who has come to rescue us, or maybe because He knew the mistreatment and abuse that had so marred my identity - kind of like a Cinderella story. This powerful picture was again restating that I am now worthy to be called His Princess. His Bride.

The surprising part was how comfortable they were. They fit perfectly, because they had been made for me. Jesus knows each of you intimately, and He knows just what will fit perfectly for you. Honestly, I would have thought He would have presented me with lacy tennis shoes, but He knew what I needed to help me to realize who He has created me to be.

The Bridegroom has made the wedding all about His Bride.

Extravagant Love

God's love is extravagant towards us. He never stops giving, because that is who He is. He promises us that He will give us beauty for ashes, gladness for mourning, praise for grief, strength for weakness, courage for fear. He turns our sorrow into great joy. That's found in Isaiah 61.

The more I am willing to open my heart with child-like faith and receive His goodness, the more I become who He has really created me to be - who He already sees me to be.

The reason it was difficult for me to take the jewelry and the crown was because I was not yet seeing myself as His Bride.

That is a process for us all which doesn't just happen overnight. We consistently renew our minds to the truth by spending intimate time with the Truth, Jesus. He is the way, the truth, and the life.

God gives us grace to be what we are already created to be.

"Grace is God's empowering presence that enables us to encounter the truth of who He really is and who we really are." - Graham Cooke[1]

Since God is timeless, He already is in our future, so He already sees who we have become.

Some time ago, I was questioning the Lord about how He could say that I was courageous when I felt like I was so full of anxiety and fear. He stopped me, and said, "The reason I can say these things about you is because they are already true."

I sucked a deep breath in as He continued. "Daughter, I can't lie, and I'm already in your future, because I'm eternal, so if I say something about you, it is because I already see who you have become. You can believe what I say about you, because it is already true of you."

This still rocks my world.

God's grace is His empowering presence in us to help us to become who He already knows us to be.

---

[1] Graham Cooke, "21st Century LifeChangers: Aglow International" © 2015 Aglow International

It is true. I can confidently wear the royal jewels and crown, because I am royalty. It has nothing to do with earning it. It is by that grace that is empowering me to be who God already says I am. Wow! Wow!

"To grant to those who mourn in Zion— to give them a beautiful headdress instead of ashes, the oil of gladness instead of mourning, the garment of praise instead of a faint spirit; that they may be called oaks of righteousness, the planting of the Lord, that he may be glorified." Isaiah 61:3 ESV

"The beginning of wisdom is this: Get wisdom, and whatever you get, get insight. Prize her highly, and she will exalt you; she will honor you if you embrace her. She will place on your head a graceful garland; she will bestow on you a beautiful crown."

Proverbs 4:7-9 ESV

"Your cheeks are lovely with ornaments, your neck with strings of jewels." Song of Solomon 1:10 ESV

Looking in the Mirror

Mirrors have always been something I've tried to avoid. That comes from the struggle I've had with identity – how I've seen myself.

Mirrors reveal to us what's on the outside, but it's what is on the inside that really matters. In fact, the way we interpret what we see in the mirror is largely a matter of perspective – the way we perceive ourselves based on the things we believe about ourselves.

Take the example of two mature twin sisters. The first woman looks in the mirror, noticing and appreciating her age marks and new grey hairs, and thinks to herself, "Thank you, Lord that I am beautifully and wonderfully made. I've earned every beautiful, grey hair." While the other twin sister looks in the mirror at the same time, and criticizes herself, thinking "Oh no, I am so ugly. I've got another wrinkle on my forehead, and more grey hair over here." They both are equally beautiful, but each see themselves through completely different lenses. It's all a matter of perspective.

Identity forms the lens we peer at the world through. If our identity is based on lies that we have believed about ourselves then our lens will be skewed. Sometimes those lies go really deep like a root system beneath a tree. It can be hard to yank them out, but Jesus is there to help us.

My identity changes based on receiving truth from God about whom He has created me to be, and then Him backing that up with experiences. The more experiences I have that back up the truth of what Jesus has said about me, the more I begin to believe it. It begins though with that small step of faith to say, "Jesus, I believe you because you said it." Then He has something to work with.

As I have experiences with Him that are based on the truth in the Bible, He rebuilds my new identity in Him. This sets in me the foundation of trust. Trust is earned, not just given. When trust has been broken so many times, by so many people, it may take time for God to rebuild trust in us. Trust is the foundation that identity is built upon.

In the vision, I was afraid of what I might see in the mirror, afraid that I would see a monster. That wasn't just an unreasonable fear to me. It was real. It was tangible. It paralyzed me at times.

When you are a child and you go through the worst of the worst with abuse, especially in situations where children are trafficked or made to participate in cultic rituals, not only is the child forced to do things that are horrific, obscene, and/or violent, they may be told what is happening is all their fault, that they are reason these things are happening. Those are common lies abusers use on children. Therefore, they may truly believe that they are evil, that they have become a monster. In other words, they may actually have a good reason to believe that they are bad, fearing they may hurt someone or themselves, even though it is lie-based.

I've heard these bellowing lies over and over again in my own head, and also from the mouths of many others who have been abused. I am not what those lies have told me, and it's not who you are either. Who God says we are is who we really are. That's why it is so important to find out our real identity in who God created us to be.

Sometimes looking into the mirror is one of the hardest things to do because it requires facing any lies you believe about yourself.

If you peer into that mirror with Jesus by your side, you can trust that He will reveal the true you – the version of who you really are created to be. It is not about how others see you or even how you see yourself, but it is about the beautiful child of God that He created you to be. The more and more I'm brave enough to peek through His lens into the mirror He gives me, the more I see who He has created me to be, and that me - she's beautiful. She's pure. She's holy. That's me!

Womb Healing – Recently, I went through an inner healing session with a new ministry, and their stance was knowing who you are called to be from Father God's heart before we ever came to Earth. God is eternal and timeless, and in Psalms 139:13-16 it says that He formed us and created us in our mother's womb, and in Ephesians 1:4-6 that He chose us before the foundation of the Earth was even created.

In the natural, we do not have the brain development for "womb memories", but while we are in the womb, our spirit is alive and well. I believe our spirit knows what is going on, feels emotions, etc., from our conception.

John the Baptist, for example, leapt in his mother's womb when Mary showed up pregnant with Jesus. In fact, Jewish women, when pregnant, would often go away for a time, as Mary did, to speak blessing over their little one in the womb, as well as protect their baby from harmful influences. They were very aware that there was a little life in their womb being formed with an understanding of who they are created to be.

After the baby is born, they can respond with joy at their mother and father's voices. Even a newborn baby has the ability to feel, to have beliefs about the world around them, and respond with emotions to voices and the things going on around them. Amazing!

Several times in my journey with the Lord, He has addressed "womb memories", or maybe better said, "womb impressions". If a child in the womb comes to believe certain things about themselves, like they are unwanted, hated, parents wanted a different gender, or maybe even the baby knew the mom tried to abort them, these things are imprinted on that child's spirit even before they even enter the world, and will affect how that child develops, until they can receive truth about who God says they are.

For me, there were things that Jesus did and spoke even in the womb that have helped me to understand that He loves me and has a beautiful plan for my life.

When Jesus held me in my mother's womb and spoke those words of destiny over me, He was reinstating the story that He had already written about me - redeeming all those negative impressions I had received when I had been conceived and growing as a fetus in the womb.

He can do the same for you. If you feel there are some deep, deep wounds regarding your identity, you can ask the true Lord Jesus to take you back and show you what you need to know, and then let Him show you how He sees you and what He said about you even before you were born. He can rewrite your story too.

I've also listed some ministries in the reference section that may help you on your healing journey.

Inner Children

My first understanding of little parts of me, or inner child work, occurred at the beginning of my inner healing journey several years ago. When my first counselor explained to me dissociation and DID (Dissociative Identity Disorder), something inside of me felt relieved and freaked out all in the same moment - relieved that someone finally understood me, and freaked out about the exposure, because now someone would know what was going on inside of me.

My internal world had been shut down, locked up, and the key to the padlock had been thrown away at a young age. Yet, as I began asking Jesus to show me what was going on, pin-thin beams of light began to penetrate any crack in my well-fortified fortresses.

Within a short time, I realized that in my complex inner world I had created to survive abuse as a child, there were little versions of me trapped in pain. They each needed help just like I have.

Dissociation is just a way the mind distracts you from something painful or encapsulates painful experiences so you can function in your day-to-day living. Someone pacing back and forth in a waiting room of a hospital is a form of dissociation. Looking at your phone a lot is said to be the adult pacifier – another form of dissociating your mind from whatever is your current reality. People do it all the time.

Yet, when something tragic happens, especially to a child, particularly if it is a form of abuse, then God gives children this amazing ability to create little parts of themselves in their minds to hold pain, or to even be present for the person while the abuse is happening, so they can go somewhere else.

Every person who has experienced this has their own survival system that they created to work for them; therefore, everyone is unique in their own little parts and how they function to help the person.

The challenge is that as the child grows into the adult and no longer needs the survival system, the system is still there running on automatic.

God knows all of this, and He knows how to reach the little ones who were created to help cope with trauma, to bring them to peace, just like He does with us. He is really good at finding them, healing them, and bringing them into a safe place where they can then be reintegrated with the core person.

Please understand, I'm not writing this from textbook knowledge, or as someone who has even studied psychology. This is all from my own experiences or the experiences of others in my life. There are many books and ministries that do fantastic jobs of explaining this concept, who have the credentials to back what they are saying, so again, check out the reference section at the end of the book or do your own research.

Eden Within

As the real Jesus has been healing my inner children and creating safe places within my heart to connect with Him, I've begun to see Him creating this place in my mind's eye that I'll call "Eden Within".

Obviously, this is a creative use of my imagination or mind's eye, but God gave us our imagination to be able to see things by faith and to be able to create new things. Every painting, every piece of artwork, every song, every house, everything we have, see, hold that has had man's invention as a part of its design began in the imagination of someone.

Many have viewed the human imagination as a negative place where mankind is tempted for evil. Yes, our mind is where we are often deceived with lies. Yet, the reason why our mind is under attack is because it is also the primary place we connect with God, where beliefs/faith are formed and solidified, and where we create with Him. Our imagination is a powerful tool.

Eden within me is this safe place that He has been creating in my inner world, in my mind's eye, that I can go with Him. I will "see" Him creating a waterfall, a green pasture, or a mountain where we can go and be together, and He will bring healing to my parts and me.

Some ministries describe this as a house inside our hearts with rooms on each different floor. For me, imagining wide-open places feels safer – like a beachfront or field of flowers. Often times, these are the type of places the Holy Spirit will lead me to see in my mind's eye, as I spend time with the Lord.

I love how God meets us where we are at, at our level of need, and brings things that are beautiful out of even our painful places. He is amazing like that.

I've also found that as I've allowed Jesus to heal my inner self, it is becoming easier and easier to connect with heavenly visions and dreams. "Eden Within" is a place of heavenly connection to God.

You too can have safe places where God will meet with you. In the natural, it may be a special place you enjoy like on a peaceful walk down a wooded path, and it also may be in your imagination, where you see the wooded path without actually being there. He loves you and desires to connect with you in ways that are meaningful to you.

"And may you, having been [deeply] rooted and [securely] grounded in love, be fully capable of comprehending with all the saints (God's people) the width and length and height and depth of His love [fully experiencing that amazing, endless love]; and [that you may come] to know [practically, through personal experience] the love of Christ which far surpasses [mere] knowledge [without experience], that you may be filled up [throughout your being] to all the fullness of God [so that you may have the richest experience of God's presence in your lives, completely filled and flooded with God Himself].

Eph. 3:17-19 AMP

Beautiful Broken Pieces

In Psalms 56:8, it says that the Lord collects our tears in a bottle. This is so precious to me, and even more so that He showed me my bottle was fused together from all the broken pieces of my life.

Many times, if we don't know what to do with the broken pieces and pain in our lives, we may try to hold on to them, even making eyeglasses out of them, to view our world through, but that will cause us to have a very skewed view of our lives, our reality, God, people, and the world around us. It's not until we ask Jesus to help us bring those broken pieces to the front and help us see those pieces of pain through His eyes, to do with them what He wants to do that He can make something new and beautiful out of them.

Simply holding on to those broken pieces may hinder our freedom. Some things I've found that hinder freedom and also skew our view are

*Holding onto grievances/debts others owe us

*Making unholy judgments and/or vows

*Believing lies

*Stuffing unprocessed emotions.

Holding Onto Grievances and Debts - This concept in scripture is probably the most commonly twisted by abusers to use against others. In writing about this, I am in no way saying that "forgiving" someone is excusing sin and/or releasing someone from the consequences of sin. I have found in my own journey that a proper, Biblical view of releasing debts is paramount in my own freedom. If I've not released offenses to God for Him to judge, especially when the offenses are great, then I've remained in some level of bondage.

In Matthew 18, where Peter asked Jesus how many times must he forgive his brother, Jesus's answer appears to instruct Peter to forgive as often as the offender asks. Then, He goes on to tell the story of the unmerciful servant. In the end, the servant who had no mercy for his fellow servant was thrown into prison until all his debt was paid.

On the surface, this may seem like Jesus is saying just let someone get away with whatever they want to do as many times as they desire as long as they say, "I'm sorry," and if you don't then you will be the one who suffers. This is a twisted view that someone may have heard from an abuser.

Jesus always is concerned about our hearts and our heart responses. In this story, the unmerciful servant sought the forgiveness of his great debt, and the King granted it. Yet, then he turned right around on his way out of the King's presence, met a fellow servant who owed him a much smaller amount of money, and not only demanded that he pay the debt in full, but then mercilessly threw his co-worker into jail.

In essence, the actions and attitude of the unmerciful servant are that of the abuser. Even though he had received great forgiveness of his debts from the King, with a hardened heart, he showed no gratitude nor mercy towards someone else. His punishment from the King was to be thrown into the very dungeon where he had thrown his co-worker, and to be tortured until he had paid all of his great debt. That's justice on the part of the King. Jesus was dealing with a wrong heart attitude on behalf of Peter.

We have been forgiven so much, so as a result our heart attitude should be one of gratefulness. We act like God when we show mercy to others as He does for us.

Holding onto debts means that I am demanding payment to me. Forgiveness is more about who will be the one who is collecting the debt. We release the debt to God for Him to collect for payment or to set free. When I chose to forgive someone, it doesn't mean that the person gets a "get out of jail free card" or that what the person did was not wrong. It simply means I am releasing the collection of the debt to the King for Him to do as He sees fit. If offenders refuse to receive the provision of the cross, then they will be judged at some point. I can trust God to be that righteous judge.

The Lord's prayer is a beautiful example of how to pray this out.

"Our Father in heaven, hallowed be your name. Your kingdom come, your will be done, on earth as it is in heaven. Give us this day our daily bread, and forgive us our debts, as we

also have forgiven our debtors. And lead us not into temptation,
but deliver us from evil." Matt. 6:9-13 ESV

For instance, I had my car broken into, and all
my possessions were stolen. I immediately felt all the
negative emotions, which were right to feel. When we
are abused, stolen from, etc., it is right to have righteous
anger, grief, sorrow, etc. In fact, Jesus said that those
who mourn will be comforted. In that moment, I
recognized the emotions, took a deep breath, and said
out loud, "Father, I forgive them. They don't know
what they are doing. I turn this over to you." Meaning,
like with Jesus on the cross, He knew they truly were
being deceived and used by the enemy like puppets.

As I released these thieves over the next several
days, a level of peace came. We still called the police
and filed a report. If they had found them, we would
have prosecuted them to the full extent of the law,
because they had broken the law. Yet, in my heart, they
didn't owe me. I turned that debt over to God, because
He is the one who is the righteous judge, and they will

eventually be held accountable for all the things they have done by Him.

My heart was free. That's the power of forgiveness. Walking in forgiveness also gives you authority to pray for others, because you have authority over what you love. You can't really love someone fully, especially those who act like your enemies, if you are holding onto the lists of debts that they owe you in your heart.

I can forgive and love someone, and yet still set healthy boundaries. I probably won't trust them, especially if they are the thieves who broke into my car. Yet, I've released them, and can see them through the eyes of the Lord.

For more on this subject, please check out my blog called "Forgiveness and Judgment" on our website, https://blossomingheartsstudio.com.

Making Unholy Judgments and Vows - There are times that judgments do need to be made. Righteous judgments result in peace and prosperity. There are many scriptures on the righteous judgments of God, and a need for honest, righteous judges in our society.

Yet again, though I judge the actions of someone as wrong, like the ring of thieves that stole my valuables were wrong in what they had done, I really can't judge the motives of their hearts behind it. That's the part of the judgment seat I let God sit in.

According to Matthew 7:1, the measure that I use to judge others is the same measure I'll be judged by. In context, I believe this is talking about judging the intent of the heart, the reason behind someone's actions, which only God can rightly do.

There are many other scriptures that call for righteous judgments to be made, and certainly there is a need for them. We suffer greatly as a society if we let corruption run free, and don't have righteous judges and judgments.

We can also pass unrighteous judgments on ourselves which can lead to pain and set ourselves up for failure in different areas of our life. Thankfully, in James 2:13, mercy triumphs over judgment. If I am a merciful person, then God promises I'll be shown mercy. I like being "mercied". Don't you?

Vows are words like "I'll never" or "I'll always", and they are based on judgments we have made. The thing about vows is that they can actually cause us to fulfill the opposite of what we vow never to be or be like. Someone who vows to never be poor like their family, will typically drive themselves towards wealth and maybe even hoarding, and though they may have material things, be very poor in other things, and/or may eventually lose everything.

Believing Lies - The lies we have believed can be held in our hearts by the things above. The enemy, the devil is the father of lies, the master deceiver, so it is his job to deceive us. Again, the more I embrace my identity of who Jesus says I am, the less deception and lies will have any effect on me, because I simply don't believe them anymore.

One of my favorite movie scenes is from a movie called "Joshua". In one scene, a widowed woman in a fitful, painful rage picks up a glass and smashes it on the ground at Joshua's feet as she pours out her painful story of losing her husband in a car accident. "This is what I am," she cries as the glass shatters. As she turns to leave, Joshua bends down and begins collecting all the pieces into his hands. As tthe camera fades from the scene, he cups the pieces with intent.

Sometime later, Joshua asked a friend to deliver a gift to the widowed woman. As she unwrapped it, she realized that all the shattered shards of the glass had been made into a beautiful, delicate ballerina. That's what Jesus does with our broken pain if we let Him. He makes beautiful things out of it.

Stuffing Unprocessed Emotions - God made us in His image, and He is an emotional God. He experiences sadness, anger, happiness, joy, etc. The only emotion He does not express is fear, because He is perfect love and perfect love casts out fear. We are made in His image, so He created us to be emotional beings. Emotions also give our lives beautiful meaning. Joy, love, compassion, excitement, etc., are all emotions that we all want to have. Feeling these positive emotions help make life worth living.

I learned a long time ago that emotions are simply our gauge inside - like a green light, yellow light, or red light - revealing to us pain that needs to be dealt with or beliefs that are wrong. If we will recognize those lights, and take our emotions to the Lord, He will help us process the reason why the light is red in a healthy way.

It may mean that we need to let out some grief and sadness, even anger or fear, in a productive process.

Grieving is an essential part of our healing journey. Naturally, grief is experienced as we work through negative emotions that come when we are hurt or experience loss, abandonment, etc. There are many things that can cause us grief such as painful loss of friendships, divorce, death, sickness, accidents, caring for others' needs, and many more things in life.

"Blessed are those who mourn, for they shall be comforted."

Matt. 5:4 ESV

The majority of our society doesn't understand the need to mourn or grieve well, and we are reaping the devastating results of pushing down trauma and covering up our emotions.

So, when the red light starts flashing, that's my cue to begin to ask the Family (Father, Son, or Holy Spirit) what's going on inside.

In the vision, Jesus took me back to a memory of my actual wedding day, at which I did fracture my foot.

I blew off the whole negative event, trying to be all I thought that was expected of me as a new wife. I acted out of obligation and pushed down all the pain, not just of my foot, but also from years of childhood abuse. I felt completely broken, ashamed, and unworthy on our wedding night, and the ache in my foot only reflected the ache in my heart.

Jesus didn't show me this to further cause me shame. He did so that He could heal it. As He spoke the truth of His great love for me in the middle of that memory, I received it, and all the shame, pain, and grief melted away. Then I was ready to walk the aisle with Him.

Many times, our next steps forward are delayed or hindered, because we have not dealt with our past. Like an invisible rope, it keeps pulling us back. Until we allow God to help us process the trauma and cut off those ties to the past (the lies, judgments, unforgiveness, and unprocessed emotions), they will hold us back. When those things are dealt with, having been properly processed, then we can freely embrace what the Lord has for us.

Some people feel that you just need to keep your eyes forward and not deal with your past. God loves our story, and He wrote a book of history called the Bible, so I'm pretty sure He is not telling us to forget our past. I believe it is more about not being bound to the pain of our past. Jesus wants to set us free from anything that we are in bondage to.

My life calling is found in Isaiah 61.

"And they shall rebuild the ancient ruins; they shall raise up the former desolations and renew the ruined cities, the devastations of many generations." Is. 61:4

When God first told me that the verse was my calling, I was in my early twenties, fresh out of college. Immediately, I imagined myself going into actual inner cities, and doing children's ministry. I had no idea how He intended for me to live out this calling – until I was years into my own inner healing journey. Then, it dawned on me that He had to rebuild my ancient ruins (my past); He had to raise up the former desolations of my family and renew my ruined cities, the devastations of my generations, before He could use me to help others to do the same thing with Him.

It is when we allow Him into our past, our story, even into the most painful parts, that He shows us Himself in it. Then it doesn't control us or hold us anymore. It becomes "His" story in us, and it becomes beautiful. God can make even the most dreadful parts of our history beautiful as we see Him in it, saving us, speaking truth to us, and redeeming all of our story.

Saying "I Do"

"For this reason, a man shall leave his father and his mother and shall be joined [and be faithfully devoted] to his wife, and the two shall become one flesh. This mystery [of two becoming one] is great; but I am speaking with reference to [the relationship of] Christ and the church." Eph. 5:31-32

This is the final step in becoming the Bride – walking down the aisle and saying, "I do." What a powerful moment in a wedding!

It is the submission of all that I am to my husband and the submission of all that He is to me – the cutting of a covenant representing continual oneness and faithfulness to another.

Marriage is when we set ourselves solely apart for another person in a covenant relationship. Holiness literally means set apart, dedicated, consecrated, and sacred. Marriage is a holy union that ultimately represents our divine covenant with the Lord.

In marriage, we are dedicating and consecrating our self to be one with another person: to love, honor, serve the other person. This is sacred. Marriage is sacred. It totally reflects the image of God. God's image is perfect oneness. Though each Person of the Godhead is separate in function and personage, yet they are completely all in perfect unity at the same time, able to seamlessly flow in and out of each other. Marriage is the closest thing we have as a picture to show what God is like. Wow! That is holy!

Because of marital union, in love, families are formed. At least, this is the way it is supposed to be. Family is a picture of the holy Trinity. When God designed family, it was with intent, to show a picture of heaven on earth.

The Bible is a book of covenant. From Genesis, to Revelation – beginning with the union of Adam and Eve in the garden to Abraham receiving the covenant of being the Father of many nations to Jesus cutting the new covenant with us through His blood shed on the cross to the Bride being married to the Bridegroom - God is about us coming into intimate, face-to-face, covenant relationship with Him.

In Exodus 19, God invited the Israelites as a nation to enter into a marriage covenant with Him. Yet, out of fear, they stood back and told Moses to go up instead, to become their representative in the covenant. They chose not to draw close to God, because they were terrified of a God who caused the mountain to burn with fire and the ground to shake. All they had known before was the iron fist of Pharaoh and the gods of Egypt. They had no concept of a loving, compassionate God who desired to make marital covenant with them.

"Now when all the people saw the thunder and the flashes of lightning and the sound of the trumpet and the mountain smoking, the people were afraid and trembled, and they stood far off and said to Moses, "You speak to us, and we will listen; but do not let God speak to us, lest we die." Moses said to the people, "Do not fear, for God has come to test you, that the fear of him may be before you, that you may not sin." The people stood far off, while Moses drew near to the thick darkness where God was." Ex.19:18-21 ESV

Moses, God's friend, veiled his face after coming down from Mt. Sinai (that intimate place of encountering God's glory), because his radiant face shone so brightly with the glory that it frightened others.

Later in the same chapter, it states that Moses regularly met with God, and each time he would have to veil his face before the people when he would come out from God's presence because of the holy, glory that shone from his face. That's a stunning image of intimate, face-to-face encounter. Yet, God longed for this relationship with them all, not just Moses.

In the new covenant, Jesus paid the dowry price for His Bride with His own blood for anyone who would say, "Yes." He tore the veil from top to bottom in half – the veil in the temple that separated the people from the Holy of Holies. He now invites us to come meet with Him face-to-face. Look at this extravagant imagery.

"Look! It is the king's marriage carriage—the love seat surrounded by sixty champions, the mightiest of Israel's host, are like pillars of protection. They stand ready with swords to defend the king and his fiancée from every terror of the night. The king made this mercy seat for himself out of the finest wood that will not decay. Pillars of smoke,

like silver mist—a canopy of golden glory dwells above it. The place
where they sit together is sprinkled with crimson. Love and mercy cover
this carriage, blanketing his tabernacle throne.
The king himself has made it for those who will become his bride.
Song of Songs 3:7-10 TPT

The mercy seat, which is sprinkled with "crimson" (the covenant blood of Jesus) is where the glory of Jehovah fills the Holy of Holies. Under the chuppah (the wedding canopy), which represents the protection, provision, and compassionate covering of a husband, dwells on that very mercy seat the Bride of Christ! His banner over the Bride is love. Wow! Can you see how vital this marriage covenant is to God?

Maybe this is why the institution of marriage is under such demonic attack in our culture. If the enemy can destroy marriage, He destroys the very image of God.

"Love is patient and kind; love does not envy or boast; it is not
arrogant or rude. It does not insist on its own way; it is not
irritable or resentful; it does not rejoice at wrongdoing but
rejoices with the truth. Love bears all things, believes all things,
hopes all things, endures all things. Love never fails."
1 Cor. 13:4-8 ESV

149

Love looks like laying down my life for someone else. Love is patient, kind, looking out for the needs of the other, long-suffering. It is being hope-filled for the future.

If you are in an abusive marriage or are a survivor of abuse, the concept of love may have been twisted up, and the idea of laying down your life for someone else may have been used against you, but this is not God's reflection of what marriage is supposed to be like.

Marriage works when both are coming into a covenant agreement to truly love one another. When one half begins to take and not give, then you have the beginnings of a failed marriage. Yet, when both are laying down their lives in love for the other, you have a beautiful oneness, a weaving of a tapestry of sacrificial love where each person lifts the other up. In this type of an environment both husband and wife thrive. It becomes a beautiful picture of heaven on earth – of family.

I also want to add here in the picture of marrying Jesus, for many that come out of abusive relationships, they can translate that into sexual terms, and be repulsed by that. Jesus is not a sexual being. He is God. He is not seeking to have sex with you. He is seeking intimacy and oneness with you, but it is on a different level than the physical act of sex, even in marriage. When Jesus kissed me in the vision (often I have a hard time with that imagery), it felt holy. It felt like pure love. It didn't feel sexual. Please go back and read Chris's heavenly encounter if you are still struggling with this.

If the idea of walking down the aisle with Jesus is hard imagery for you, especially in our country where everything is so sexualized, remember that Jesus is extremely respectful of that and knows the things we struggle with. He doesn't push past our boundaries. He always respects our freewill, and He will meet you where you need Him.

Jesus is one with the Father and the Holy Spirit. They invite us into oneness with Them now, in the present. Yet, there is also coming a day for the marriage of the Lamb (Jesus) with the Bride of Christ. This is a more corporate marriage – a marriage of Jesus Christ to His Church.

The point here is that Jesus desires deep intimacy with us as His bride now. If we will yield to this holy matrimony, we can and will walk from a place of victory in Him, hand in hand, side by side. It is a powerful, redeemed, holy place to live life from - a place of covenant with the God of the Universe under His canopy of love. His banner over me is love. The veil has been lifted. We can now meet with Him face-to-face. He is kissing us with His holy love and asks us to walk forward with Him from here.

Is there a battle to fight? Yes. A fierce battle at times. Yet our position from where we fight is everything.

Prepared for Battle

So, the battle is raging around, and we need to suit up and remain in our armor. Our battle is not against flesh and blood, but against this present darkness, against principalities and powers. (Eph. 6:2)

In Jesus, as His Bride, we have already won, because He won us at the cross. He paid the ultimate marriage dowry. He paid the price to purchase us from darkness, from the grips of the enemy, and to bring us into the new kingdom of His Father, the Great I Am.

In the course of my life, I've listened to many, many teachings on the armor of God. I can recite the pieces, and even sing songs about them. We spent twenty years teaching children's church, and one of the main topics we taught them was the armor of God as found in Ephesians 6. For a five-year-old, that armor was a very real thing. They would dress up in the plastic armor suit, and pretend to knock away foam, flaming arrows that the devil threw their way. Our real armor is far more amazing than that.

In the true battle, the enemy is real, his lies very convincing, and his arrows flaming. Lies, deception, hatred, division, fear, manipulation, and control are all very real weapons used against us.

This part of the bridal journey was unexpected for me. I was caught up in the aroma of roses, after all. Yet, the Lord Jesus knows what is coming. He wants us to walk in victory. His direction was to suit up.

One thing that fascinated me was that there was no need to take off the bridal clothes. In fact, it is essential that we keep them on. It is a representation of our intimacy in our holy communion with the Lord. This has to be the core of where our life flows.

At first, I thought He meant for me to take off the wedding dress, the shoes, etc., but joy rose as He said that I was to put on the armor over them; that in fact, the armor had been fashioned just for me, a perfect fit.

It reminds me of the story of David as he prepared to fight Goliath. The king wanted David to wear his armor, the man-made armor of a worldly, cowardly king. David chose the weapons of a slingshot, a stone, and the faith in his God. His clothing was praise, his shield was faith, and his weapons were simple, but mighty in God to the taking down of giants.

As we put on the breastplate of righteousness (our right standing with God), the belt of truth (the truth of who God is and who He has called me to be – the truth of His Word), the helmet of salvation (which fits right in with our crown), the shoes of peace (fitted perfectly over the wedding slippers), the shield of faith (our confident trust in our Husband), and our sword of the Spirit (which is our sharp, offensive weapon against the enemy), we are covering ourselves with the heavenly armor that helps us not only to stand up, but to advance against the enemy and his devices. It enables us to walk in the authority Jesus has given us.

We have authority, because we are married to Jesus, the Son of God. Our authority comes through our holy union with Him. This is not because we have it all together or are perfect. It's not about us at all. It's about what Jesus has accomplished through the new covenant, which He made possible for us through the cross. When we say yes to Him, to receiving Him, it is like signing our name to a marriage certificate. When I sign a document in my name, I carry the authority from my unity with my husband. All the authority he has, I now also have, because I sign the same last name. This doesn't take away from my identity. It enhances it. Because my husband's name is an honorable one, it is a blessing to carry my husband's name.

We carry the honorable, highly exalted name of Jesus. Wow!

Just like Jesus said our trust in Him has to be exercised. We can't leave our shield of faith on the ground. We pick it up, and in obedience, we use it. Trusting and resting in His love for us is one of the most powerful forms of warfare. It protects our joy. As He laughs at our enemy, we step forward in His love. We embrace a confident trust in His love for us. Wow! Wow!

My favorite part of the armor was the sword. As the words changed each time that I flipped the sword over, it mesmerized me. It is the sword of the Spirit. It is the spoken Word of God – truth in love. It is praise. It is intercession. It is sharper than any other sword. It's the power of our testimony. In each situation, the Spirit will direct us how to war with it, because the Spirit leads it.

I am fighting some battles right now that have felt so fierce at times. Sometimes, it feels completely overwhelming. Sometimes, it is wise to stop and process some emotions. Even in that, I grieve in hope. I process out my emotions with Jesus to get to the other side of it. I hide in Him, under the canopy of His love. I rest in the intimacy I have with Him. He and I fight the good fight with love as my primary weapon for nothing can ever overcome love.

It's not always easy. In fact, many times it's not. We can live from a place of joy, a place of love, a place of victory in Him from the bridal place of intimacy, because He has already won.

Shields up! Swords Out!

The Warrior Bride

As I walked off of the labyrinth, I encountered two creatures in the vision. This may seem like odd imagery to you. In Revelation, you will find lots of imagery that is a bit different. I do not equal my experiences with the written word of God, but I do give it value, and I ask the Holy Spirit for confirmation if it is from the Lord. In this case, God clearly gave me that. I also am not in any way suggesting that either of these animals are spirit guides. They represented things that I needed and/or part of who God is.

The Lion of the Tribe of Judah — I've always loved, loved the story of the "Chronicles of Narnia" by CS Lewis. As a child, I'd dream of escaping to Aslan's land through a secret portal. Funny thing is I still do. Except now, Aslan is the Lion of the Tribe of Judah, and His kingdom is the heavenly kingdom that I engage in and from.

The veil is so thin. His kingdom is all around us and in us - just a step through the "Eden Within" into His heavenly kingdom.

Some say that we are entering into the time, the season of the Lion of the Tribe of Judah, the time that the Great King is returning. Jesus is the Lion of the Tribe of Judah.

Sometimes, Jesus will appear to us in different forms in our mind's eye, and for many, He appears to them in dreams and/or visions. He often has appeared to me as that great lion in visions in my mind. In this vision, I still remember the warmth of His fur as I stroked and hugged His strong neck. He has never used His strength against me. Always for me. His love is strong. He is strong for us!

One of my favorite scenes from "Prince Caspian" (a book in CS Lewis's series of The Chronicles of Narnia) is when Lucy meets Aslan in the forest begging for His help. With a fierce compassion, Aslan peers deep into Lucy's eyes. "Now you are a lioness," said Aslan. "And now all Narnia will be renewed. But come. We have no time to lose."

She stood to face the enemy with a little dagger, because the Lion of the Tribe of Judah was standing beside her. Her strength and confidence came from knowing by experience the ONE who was with her.

Visualizing Jesus as the Lion of the Tribe of Judah brings strength and courage to me. Knowing He is padding beside me brings peace in that He is always with me, and He has won the victory.

The Snowy White Owl - Sometimes, the Lord has redeemed things or images for me that I thought meant evil. Owls have been one of those creatures that I have had negative connotations of. For many years, I thought of owls as something that the occult would use as a way to curse you. If an owl showed up, it meant something bad or evil was about to happen.

A few weeks prior to this conference, I had been in a prayer meeting and our leader was talking about how in her mind's eye, sometimes she could envision herself flying on an eagle with Jesus above all the things of the world, and she could see the strategies of the enemy so that we would be able to pray against them.

When I heard her say that in my heart I prayed, "Lord, I want an eagle too."

At which point, I clearly heard inside. "No, child. Not an eagle. An owl."

I thought I was hearing an evil voice, but it really sounded like the Lord. I wrestled with this for a couple of weeks, but consistently owls kept coming up. On one of our homeschooling days, I picked up a new magazine my animal-loving daughter had received in the mail. Inside, the featured animal was a snowy, white owl.

As I read it, the Lord began to speak to me again. "Snowy white owls fly as high as the eagles do, they nest where the eagles nest, they fly and hunt by day and night, and the mothers are fiercely protective of their young." The Lord paused. "You are like this to me. I want you to have a snowy white owl to ride on. I don't give you things that are evil. I'm a good father."

When I looked to the left of me in the vision, and saw the snowy white owl bigger than me, it was one the most profound things I've ever seen. It was so real to me that its light, puffy feathers tickled my fingers as I lifted my hand through them. As it peered straight into my eyes, I saw strength, determination, fierce love, the fire of God, and wisdom. My heart leapt with anticipation.

What I felt the Lord was revealing to me is that this owl represented characteristics of good things that He was developing in me. The snowy, white owl was one aspect of a picture of who He was creating me to be. In doing so, He completely redeemed the meaning and imagery of the owl for me. Owls are His creation. They are meant to be majestic creatures that represent His wisdom, glory, and so much more. He redeems the things the enemy has tried to pervert. For some others, perhaps it may represent the Holy Spirit or aspects of the Holy Spirit's work in us.

Including this part of the vision is for you to understand two things. First of all, God wants to redeem things in your life that may seem like a curse or bad. He can and will make all things new. Secondly, sometimes God may use images that might stretch you a little bit or might be a bit out of the box, but He will confirm it is from Him through lining up with His character and nature found in the Bible. In receiving of those things, He reveals to you, you might just find new discoveries of wonder with Him, like I did that day.

My friends, some may think that these experiences are only for a few or certainly not for them, but I really believe these experiences are for everyone. In fact, Judith, the artist who is also featured in this book is from a different continent than I am; yet, when she read my unpublished version, she expressed how the owl part had really spoken to her, and how God had been also speaking to her about owls. She immediately "saw" the drawing that needed to be put in. I can't make that up.

He knows you better than you can ever imagine and loves you even more than that. If you are paying attention and are willing, there are so many ways He wants to have an intimate friendship with you. He loves to connect with you in so many creative ways that are meaningful to you.

He is a good, good father who so desires for us to engage with Him and to know His heart of love for us. Through our intimacy with the true, Lord Jesus, He will pour His Spirit out through us to a world that so desperately needs Him.

Arm in Arm

These are the words Jesus left me with as I stepped off that day. And again, I leave them with you now.

"We will walk this out together, arm in arm, from this place of intimacy, with my authority, because it all belongs to you. You have my name now. All my authority is given to you, because you are married to me. Everything I have is yours. Everything you have is mine. You are mine and belong to me. Dream with me now!"

Extra Confirmation

To ensure I would not chalk all that happened up to an overactive imagination, which I was tempted to do, one of my prayer buddies from home texted me the following scripture verses shortly after I had completed my journey on the labyrinth.

As I read her text message on my phone that day, I almost dropped it from shock.

"I was up early this morning praying for you, that you would see yourself as the Bride. The Lord had me focus on this scripture in Isaiah 61:10 '...he has clothed me with the garment of salvation; he has covered me with the robe of righteousness, as a bridegroom decks himself like a priest with a beautiful headdress, and as a bride adorns herself with her jewels,' and Romans 13:11-12 '...put on the armor of light.'"

May you also experience the fullness of what it means to be the Bride of Christ.

"The Spirit and the Bride say, "Come."" Rev. 22:17

RESOURCES

The following is a list of ministries that you may find helpful on your own heart healing journey. I don't necessarily endorse everything offered through these ministries, but what I've seen and experienced has been beneficial.

Art Sozo: https://artsozo.com

Christopher Carter (author): https://discovertheheavens.org

Called to Peace Ministries: https://calledtopeace.org

Elijah House Ministries: https://elijahhouse.org

Ellel Ministries: https://ellel.org

Heart Sync Ministry: https://heartsyncministries.org

Rebecca Davis (author) and her book series on Untwisting

Scriptures: https://heresthejoy.com

Immanuel Approach Ministry: https://immanuelapproach.com

International Society of Deliverance

Ministers: https://isdministers.org

Transformations Class: https://kingdomequippingcenter.org

Lisa Meister's (author): "You've Got the Wrong Guy" available on

Amazon, and her podcast, https://anchor.fm/lisa-meister

Judith Kayadoe (artist): https://royaltyfineart.com

Oaks Rising: https://oaksrising.com

Restoration in Christ Ministry: https://rcm-usa.org

Sapphire Leadership Group: https://theslg.com

Transformation Prayer Ministry https://transformationprayer.org

Wendy Cohen: https://houseofbeauty.org

ABOUT THE AUTHOR

Carolyn "Charismata" Weaver
Author, Artist, and Healing Art Coach

My nickname "Charismata" came from an encounter with Jesus where I asked Him what He called me in heaven. He often calls us things that we can't even believe for at the time. That was the case for me. The name means "power of His glory". At the time He first called me that, I was probably the weakest I had ever been, as I struggled through an intense inner healing process. It was in those valleys of Him healing my deepest wounds from childhood abuse that I came to hear His voice clearly and see Him in the spirit. My passion now is to point others to that same place of healing and intimacy.

I'm married to an amazingly patient and loving man who keeps me grounded, and I have three children. I love to write about my journey with the Lord and enjoy sharing the creative process with others - how it can help you connect with God and bring healing.

For more information about what our healing art classes, other books, artwork, and more, please check out www.blossomingheartsstudio.com.

Made in the USA
Monee, IL
23 November 2022